Agatha Christie's
POIROT

◆

A CELEBRATION OF
THE GREAT DETECTIVE

PETER HAINING

LWT

BOXTREE

First published in Great Britain in 1995 by Boxtree Limited,
Text © Boxtree/LWT 1995
Written by Peter Haining
Photographs © LWT 1995

10 9 8 7 6 5 4 3 2 1

Designed by Clare Truscolt
Colour Origination by Jade Reproductions
Printed and bound in the United Kingdom by
Cambus Litho Ltd, East Kilbride, for
Boxtree Limited
Broadwall House
21 Broadwall
London SE1 9PL

A CIP catalogue entry for this book is available from the
British Library.

ISBN: 0 7522 1046 7

The publishers would like to thank the following: BBC Picture
Archives for photos on pp. 61, 62 and 63, © BBC; the *Daily
Telegraph* for the extract on p. 38, © The Telegraph plc,
London, 1975; Lumiere Pictures Ltd. for photos on pp. 102, 103,
105–9 and 113, © Lumiere Pictures Ltd.; Mander and
Mitchenson theatre collection of photos on pp. 35 and 93
courtesy of Mander and Mitchenson; the Mirror Syndication
for photo on p. 66, © Mirror Syndication International;
Turner Entertainment for photo on p. 99, © Turner
Entertainment Ltd.

Agatha Christie's
POIROT

Other Television tie-ins by the same author

On Call with Doctor Finlay
On Duty with the Chief
On the Rounds with Medics

CONTENTS

THE FAMILY VIEW OF POIROT

Over a span of more than forty years, Agatha Christie wrote nearly forty books featuring Hercule Poirot; in the 1930s and 1940s alone he appeared no less than twenty times! It will therefore come as no surprise that, fond as Agatha Christie was of her little Belgian detective when he first appeared in *The Mysterious Affair at Styles* in 1921, that affection began to wear a little thin as she pounded out, at her public's and her publisher's insistence, book after book containing the little man! Small wonder that in desperation in, I think, 1948, she wrote *Curtain*, but was then submerged with pleas from her family, publishers and business advisers not to allow it to be published, to which she eventually responded. *Curtain* was eventually published in 1975.

By the time I was around, irritation had been mitigated again by affection and she had been mollified by the enthusiastic reception which some books without Poirot had received. She had also, as it were, recharged her batteries by writing some more romantic novels under the name of Mary Westmacott. During the 1950s and 1960s Poirot is more circumspect in the number of his appearances and everybody became much more relaxed about him.

But then we had all to face the terrible problem of his visual appearance – what to do about him in films? Agatha Christie herself was extremely nervous about him appearing, because she was convinced that all her readers would have whatever image they had of their beloved Poirot shattered. Therefore, I think she had reservations about all the people who played him in her lifetime. The last portrayal she saw was Albert Finney in *Murder on the Orient Express*. She was bowled over with admiration for the lavish attention to detail in the film and for Albert Finney's professionalism, and I think she thought he was one of the best. She never saw, of course, Peter Ustinov or David Suchet.

Personally, I regret very much that she never saw David Suchet. I think that visually he is much the most convincing, and perhaps he manages to convey to the viewer just enough of the irritation that we always associate with the perfectionist to be convincing. Certainly I feel that over the last five years we have come closer, thanks to LWT, Brian Eastman and everyone else involved, to a visual realisation of one of the great detective creations of the century.

Mathew Prichard 1995

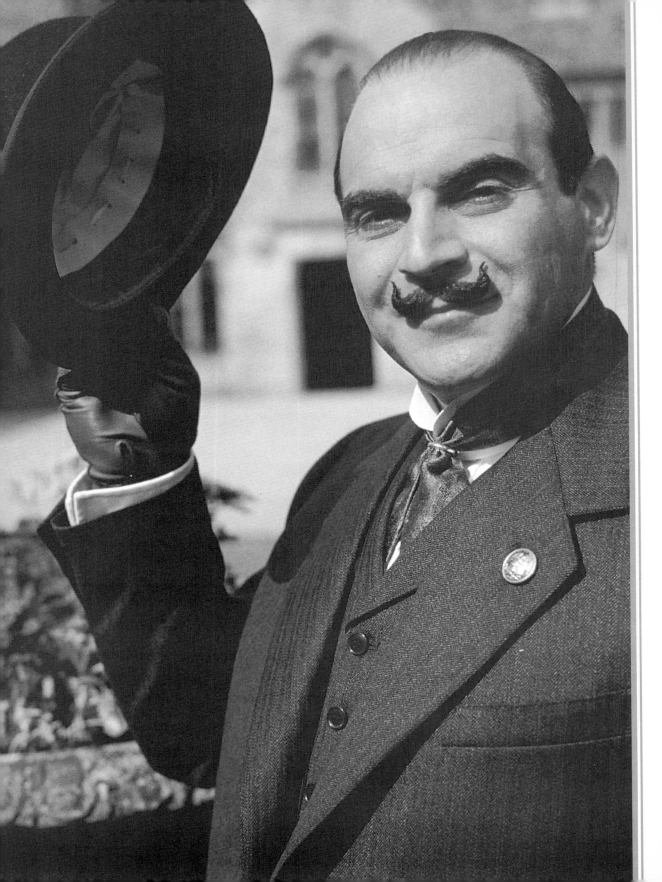

THEY DO IT WITH CAMERAS *

Poirot was an extraordinary looking little man. He was hardly more than five feet, four inches, but carried himself with great dignity. His head was exactly the shape of an egg, and he always perched it a little on one side. His moustache was very stiff and military. The neatness of his attire was almost incredible, I believe a speck of dust would have caused him more pain than a bullet wound. Yet this quaint dandified little man who, I was sorry to see, now limped badly, had been in his time one of the most celebrated members of the Belgian police. As a detective, his flair had been extraordinary, and he had achieved triumphs by unravelling some of the most baffling cases of the day.

In these words, published seventy-five years ago in a book entitled *The Mysterious Affair at Styles*, a young writer in her first crime novel named Agatha Christie introduced a detective who was destined for immortality. Neither she, nor the reviewers or readers who picked up copies of the 2,500 first printing of the book bearing the publisher's name, 'John Lane, London & New York', had any idea that a legend which would, in time, spread to the radio, onto the stage, and then into films and television, had begun. One reviewer, the anonymous scribe of the London *Evening News* perhaps had an inkling, writing in his column, 'It is with congratulation to Mrs Christie and to the large contingent of admirers of the detective novel that I make the announcement that in this writer there is a distinguished addition to the list of writers in this genus'.

Much has happened to M. Hercule Poirot in the intervening three

* With apologies to the title of the Miss Marple novel, *They Do It With Mirrors* (1952).

Opposite:
Poirot personified by
David Suchet.

quarters of a century. The thirty-three novels and ten volumes of short stories about him have been translated into approximately forty-four languages and sold uncounted millions of copies. He has been portrayed on the stage by actors as disparate as Charles Laughton, Francis L. Sullivan and Patrick Cargill; in the cinema by stars like Austin Trevor, Tony Randall, Albert Finney and Peter Ustinov; and on television by Harold Huber, Martin Gabel and Ian Holm.

Yet it has taken all of this time to find a definitive Poirot, an actor capable of bringing to the screen this enigmatic and extraordinary figure who has been called the greatest lateral thinking detective in crime fiction. But by general consent, in the LWT (London Weekend Television) programme *Agatha Christie's Poirot* starring David Suchet, the little Belgian-born sleuth is at last being seen as his creator might have hoped — accurate to her descriptions of him and in cases faithful to her stories.

Much, also, has happened to the legend of Agatha Christie herself, who died peacefully in January 1976, revered as 'The Queen of Crime'. For that first book she earned the princely sum of £25, but such was her appeal to readers all over the world — due to her subsequent novels about Poirot, Miss Jane Marple, Tommy and Tuppence Beresford, *et. al*, that at the time of her death she was one of the very few authors to command advances in excess of $1 million from American publishers *alone* for the paperback rights to her works.

But this is a book about the acclaimed TV series which was launched in 1989, and now six years later enjoys such popularity with viewers and has taken such a hold on the public imagination that there is every indication it will continue for as long a period again — until, in fact, all the cases of Hercule Poirot are exhausted. The success is one that owes much to a team of people who have in the main remained with the series since its inception — in particular the producer, Brain Eastman; the script consultant, Clive Exton; and the stars, David Suchet, Hugh Fraser, Philip Jackson and Pauline Moran. It is their achievement which this book celebrates.

The story begins with one man's dream, another man's dedication to authenticity and some inspired casting — especially the man who plays the little Belgian sleuth, and whose looks and persona have proved beyond the reach of his predecessors in the part.

Producer Brian Eastman is a much-respected figure in television circles. A lean, forceful personality, Brian exudes enthusiasm for Poirot, which he films under the umbrella of his company, Carnival Films & Theatre Ltd, for London Weekend Television. It was at LWT's offices in the South Bank Television Centre overlooking the Thames that he talked about the making of a notable TV landmark.

Brian Eastman, mastermind of the LWT series.

David Suchet, the consummate professional on set.

Among Brian's earlier productions have been two award-winning series based on books by the humorous writer Tom Sharpe, *Porterhouse Blue* and *Blott on the Landscape*; the LWT series, *Forever Green* with John Alderton and Pauline Collins; and in complete contrast, the semi-futuristic series, *Bugs*, for the BBC. Although Brian admits to having been a Christie reader since his youth, the inspiration for the Poirot series came about in a most improbable way – as a result of *Blott on the Landscape*, made in 1986, in which David Suchet played an eccentric handyman complete with beret and small moustache.

'That was the first time I had worked with David, Brian explains, where the idea of doing Poirot all started. Just after we had finished making Blott I met Rosalind Hicks, Agatha's daughter. She said to me, 'That chap you've just worked with, David Suchet, he'd make a wonderful Poirot!' Although the idea for the series was in the back of my mind, it was Rosalind who really suggested it and deserves the credit.

'So I went back to David and said, 'Look, the Christie Estate think you could make a terrific Poirot. I'd like to do it. What do you think?' Well, I could tell he was very intrigued by the idea and everything really went from there. David is an actor I have always admired, particularly in the role of an anglicised foreigner. He has a wonderful ability to pick on the idiosyncrasies of the British character and turn them to use as a foreigner.'

Brian is equally quick to point out that although he isn't a member of the Agatha Christie fan club he *is* an admirer of her work and sensed its potential for television.

'It is really only since I have worked on the material that I have come to love the stories and appreciate how skilful she was and what incredible variety she manage to introduce into them. Apart from the novels and short stories about Poirot, think of all the other material she wrote! The formula she uses is quite consistent, however. Yet within it, the sort of crimes that are committed, the way they are done, the people who do them, their motives and the situations in which they occur are almost endlessly varied. As a result we have a formula with which we are comfortable – and within it there are always so many different things going on all the time. It's one of the reasons why the series has been able to go on so long, I believe.'

With the blessing of Agatha Christie's daughter, and with his star already in mind, Brian was next faced with adapting the stories for television. He had no hesitation in making his choice – Clive Exton, a veteran film and TV writer, whose previous work had included a number of literary adaptations and who was known to like detective stories.

'I've always been a Christie fan,' says Clive, a genial, expressive man, 'and so it was a great delight to be asked to adapt the Poirot cases. Initially, we were only going to use the short stories, but once the series took off we soon got into the novels as well. Although I did most of the early episodes, the work-load soon became such that we had to build up a team of writers. Several of them, like Anthony Horowitz and Douglas Watkinson, have now been with us for quite a while. They know Poirot inside and out.'

Clive, whose own knowledge of the canon is certainly second to none, came to script writing via a career in advertising in the late Forties, after which he tried for a time to be an actor.

'I was a very bad actor,' he admits candidly, with a laugh, 'and I had very little faith in the productions I was appearing in. Things came to a head when I was doing this play, *Paddle Your Own Canoe*, which was a translation from the French, and it was awful. I'd been doing it for about two years when I said to my wife, 'I could write something better than this rubbish.' And she said, 'Well, in that case you'd better do it.' So I did.

'My first play was called *No Fixed Abode* (1959) and it was produced by Granada. It was very well received and so I decided to give up acting there and then. I've now been writing for films and television for the last thirty years!'

No Fixed Abode was followed by several other memorable single plays including *Soldier* and *The Trial of Dr Fancy*, plus film scripts for a number of successful crime thrillers including *Night Must Fall* (1963), *10 Rillington Place* (1970) and *Nightmare Park* (1973). He has also been associated with another top ITV series, the *Ruth Rendell Mysteries*, for which he scripted the episodes 'Wolf To The Slaughter' and 'Guilty Thing Surprised'.

When Clive began work on the scripts for Poirot, Brian Eastman already had a very clear vision about the period of time in which he wanted to set the stories.

The producer takes up the story again. 'When we started, our episodes were all based on short stories, and had to be adapted to fit a one-hour spot. Now as you know, Agatha's writing life falls into pre-war and post-war periods – not that there is much difference in the styles. But to me there was something about all her writing which felt pre-war. Even in the books written in the Fifties and Sixties she did not alter her method of construction – she certainly altered her characters and the environments they were in – but essentially they had this pre-war feel, despite the fact they were dealing with post-war characters and subjects. So for that reason I felt it was important to start the series in a pre-war setting. We were also helped by the fact that many of the short stories fitted very neatly into that time frame.'

Brian says that he has always been a strong believer that any television series should be very specific about the period of time in which it is set.

'You don't necessarily have to put a date up on the screen to say that this is such and such a year,' he elaborates. 'But those making the series must be very sure themselves about the time, so that the point gets through to the viewer. For this reason, when we were deciding on a date for Poirot we looked through all the aspects of the Thirties –

Authentic Thirties artefacts have been a feature of the series.

design, transport, the state of the police, all those sorts of things – and came to the conclusion that 1936 would be a *very* good year!'

A glance at the newspapers for 1936 quickly reveals that it was, indeed, a year of drama and change. On the world stage, the Nazis had goose-stepped into the Rhineland and Civil War had broken out in Spain. In Britain it was to be the year Edward VIII gave up the throne for love of Mrs Simpson; the Queen Mary sailed on her maiden voyage; and the Spitfire fighter aircraft went on display for the first time. It was a significant year in the media, too: new film studios were opened at Pinewood, and in August television was demonstrated live for the first time to over 7,000 visitors to Olympia.

Clive Exton, who was a party to this decision, comments: 'We chose 1936 for a number of reasons – not the least being that it seemed to fit so well with Poirot's character. It also transpires that by 1936 almost all of the modern inventions that subsequently became part of our lives in the Fifties and Sixties had been designed, and it was only the military and economic crisis of the Second World War which brought everything to a halt. Take the roads for one example – the M1 was designed in 1936 but not actually built until 1956! In a way the mid- to late-Thirties were an incredibly flourishing and futuristic period – and Poirot

Death in the Clouds was filmed in the Roland Garros stadium in Paris.

David Suchet with
co-stars Hugh Fraser and
Philip Jackson.

was a man who was very interested in such things.'

Brian Eastman seconds this view. 'It was very much a watershed period of history. There were these elements of modernity set in a pre-war period which provided such a wonderful contrast. And when you combined this with a man, Poirot, who is interested in modern things but in terms of his dress and appearance is almost a pre-First World War figure, the contrast is even more striking. So 1936 became the driving force of the way we designed the series – the look of the costumes, the styles of architecture, and so on.'

The other way in which we have been very specific about the year is by mentioning real events. Here I admit we are taking a bit of a liberty with Agatha's work, because she did not do that in her stories. But we felt that such references would make the series *feel* very real. As a result almost every film contains at least one event of that year.

'We do allow ourselves a little bit of license,' Brian confesses. 'Sometimes we take an event from 1935 and sometimes from 1937 – but pretty much within a twelve- to fifteen-month period. There have been occasions when these events have formed an integral part of the story. Take *Death in the Clouds* as an example. We actually set that around the 1936 Paris Open French Tennis Tournament which Fred Perry won during his Grand Slam year. We hired an actor to impersonate Fred and filmed at the Roland Garros courts.

'It was just a way of getting into the story, but the sequence gave it great veracity. I think that one of the reasons why viewers have responded so well to the show is because, almost without realising it, they know that they are watching a fictional man in fictional situations, but they believe in his world through the mention of things about which they have heard. So instead of being entirely fanciful, the series has a foot in reality.'

Having decided that authenticity was to be a vital keynote of the series, Brian made another decision about casting and the kind of actors he wanted to use.

'Famous faces can detract from authenticity,' he explains, 'and though some undoubtedly do draw people to a show, the viewer can easily end up watching an actor or actress more than who they are playing or what they are doing. So apart from David Suchet, we deliberately did not cast 'names', although we have subsequently used some well-known guest stars in single episodes and the two-hour specials.'

The uniting of Suchet with Hugh Fraser as Captain Hastings in the partnership which has many of the same elements as the Holmes and Watson friendship has since proved to be another important contribution to the success of the series. Just as Philip Jackson's Inspector Japp – the Lestrade to the Holmes-Watson team – has given the policeman a higher profile than he had in the original stories. Pauline Moran's achievement as Miss Lemon has been to transform an ordinary secretary into a living character.

But central to the success of the series has undoubtedly been David Suchet's development of the role for which Rosalind Hicks thought he was so well suited. David's now seemingly effortless performances have not, though, been achieved without a great deal of research and hard work. Brian Eastman has a particularly vivid memory of one instance of this dedication that occurred before the series went into

The making of a great screen partnership - David Suchet and Hugh Fraser.

The famous Poirot 'walk' in action.

production.

'We shot quite a lot of test material to help David get his characterisation right,' he recalls. 'I remember sitting in a viewing theatre with him watching lots of different takes showing him walking down a street away from camera. We were trying to find the way Poirot walks. We actually both leapt up together when this one take came up. 'That's it!' we both shouted. David had finally got Poirot's step right, the way he carries his left hand clasped behind his back and how he holds his bottom. He has this very tight little manoeuvre – but without any gay quality to it. I think that walk really sums up the character.'

Poirot's moustache was, if anything, an even more important element in David's development of the character, as he himself explains later in the book. Brian, too, has his own memories of what he describes as a 'constant battle' with the little sleuth's facial adornment.

'It's quite extraordinary,' he smiles, 'David will arrive at the studio or on location as himself, but the moment he goes into make-up and puts the moustache on he becomes Poirot! I can walk in to talk to him about something that may have nothing to do with the series, but he'll answer me as Poirot. He just can't help himself because he's *become* the character!

The troublesome
moustache in close-up.

Painstaking care is
taken with David Suchet's
make-up.

'If you were to look at that moustache over the whole series, you'd see that it has changed shape and size rather more times than we would care to admit. The trouble is that it's not a precise art. We order the moustaches from a specialist makers – one for each episode of a series – and they come in slightly different shapes and sizes. Our make-up people obviously work on them to try and get them to look the same, but there have been times when I've not been on the set and watched the rushes the following day and seen that the moustache hasn't looked right. So we've then had to go back and film the whole scene again!

'The trouble is that even though there is this complex plot going on and lots of other characters about, the bulk of the audience are riveted by what's on David's lip. If it just doesn't look right – and particularly if it doesn't look consistent with the way it did in the rest of that particular film – people are not going to be saying, 'Oh, I wonder how so-and-so was murdered?' No, they'll be looking at Poirot's moustache and saying, 'Look – it's changed shape! ' It may only be a small object, but it bedevils us all the time.'

It is not only viewers who are fixated with Poirot's moustache. *The Guardian's* television critic, Nancy Banks-Smith, devoted a whole column to 'The Mysterious Moustache Affair' in January 1989, writing, 'The subject we have to address today is one of crime's strangest unsolved mysteries. What *kind* of moustache did Hercule Poirot wear? Was it a dizzying succession of interlocking circles like an exploding watch? Did it leap out left and right like wild horses trying to tear him apart? Did it stay aloft by its own built-in bounce or was it artificially assisted? Or was it the laughably small moustache affected by David Suchet in *Hercule Poirot's Casebook*?'

After examining the various descriptions of the moustache in Agatha's books right from the Twenties through to the Seventies, Nancy conceded that it was a question probably impossible to resolve.

'Immense, enormous, magnificent, luxuriant are the most commonly recurring words,' she concluded, and then joined the rest of her colleagues in praising the show: 'The series is charmingly in period and Suchet's performance, unlike the moustache, magnificent.'

David, for his part, defends his trade mark vigorously. 'It's a work of art, neat, symmetrical, tidy, crisp, a thing of beauty – yes. But ridiculous

– *no!*' he says firmly. 'I get annoyed when people say it is absurd, which is not correct. In the 1930s waxed moustaches were highly fashionable, and Poirot's is quite modest by the standards of the time. It was a bit spectacular to begin with – the tips were almost touching my nose at one time – but it has been trimmed down a bit since then.'

The arguments about the moustache notwithstanding, David has been even more surprised by the letters he has received suggesting that Poirot is a sex symbol to many women viewers.

'I don't know whether it is the moustache which turns women viewers on,' David says with a slightly puzzled grin, 'but they do warm to him. A lot of the letters I get are from women who want to look after Poirot, for although he's very self-sufficient, he is also slightly vulnerable. I think they see him being so fussy on screen and so organised that it becomes a challenge to try and take him over.

'I know from reading Agatha Christie's books that Poirot was sad he never married. In fact, he did love women, and especially English girls who made him fluffy omelettes!'

Two actresses who have appeared as the nearest thing to love interests in the series have their own ideas about Poirot's sex appeal.

Red-headed Kika Markham, who played the beautiful Russian Countess Vera Rossakoff who is also a jewel thief in the 1991 version of *The Double Clue*, says, 'He's the sort of man every woman wants to change. They see him as a challenge. They want to get behind his formal exterior and see what raging passions lurk beneath his waistcoat.

'In the original stories about the countess she is described as the one great love in his life. For that reason I felt that there should be a more open show of affection between them on the screen. I thought it would be natural for me to put my hand on his shoulder and then perhaps kiss him on the cheek – but I was told that it wasn't allowed. I *did* get to kiss him on the forehead, though, and that was only because I discovered it's how Russians behave when they are saying goodbye to someone close.'

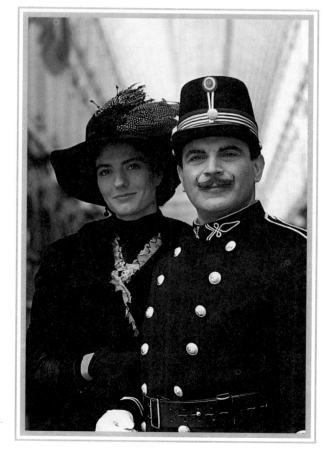

The young Poirot and his early love, Virginie Mesnard (Anna Chancellor) in *The Chocolate Box*.

Countess Vera Rossakoff
(Kika Markham) the
'great love' of Poirot's life.

Anna Chancellor, who played the pretty Virginie Mesnard in *The Chocolate Box* in which Poirot was seen as a dapper young policeman in Brussels, has another view.

'He is always chivalrous and polite, with a strict code of conduct,' she says. 'He makes a lady feel like a lady. He always opens doors, walks on the correct side of the pavement and is the quintessential gentleman. There could never be any problems. A mischievous twinkle and perhaps a kind-hearted flirtation, but never a threat.'

Anna appeared as the girl whom the young Poirot fell for, not because she was a female in distress but because she shared his sense of honesty.

'She shared his strong sense of right and wrong and a burning quest for truth. They got on well because they both enjoyed the chase and finding out the truth. She was also brave, fearless and stood up for what she believed in – which was unusual for that era.'

Brussels, in fact is just one of many locations that have been used during the making of the series, though the majority have been in southern England, with Twickenham Studios the most frequently used place for interior scenes. Another distinctive element of the programme is the title sequence, which surely ranks as one of the most original on TV.

The sequence, which mixes live action, traditional and computer animation techniques, was the handiwork of Graphic designer Pat Gavin, a longtime employee of LWT and renowned in the industry for his seminal titles for the *South Bank Show*. Although the titles only last sixty-four seconds, the mood of Thirties decorative Cubism and the title *Poirot* appearing out of the wheels of a Mallard train engine took months to prepare and film.

'I couldn't have done the effects with any conventional optical system,' Pat says of the brilliant sequence which finally cost almost £50,000. 'I wouldn't have been able to do the airbrush with that degree of control, or build up the twenty-five layers without multiple processing. I've always been terrified by the mathematics of computers, but working on the titles for Poirot using a unique computerised, film-based system changed all that. I think the end product was worth all the trouble.'

Certainly there was an immediate impact when the first episode of Poirot, *The Adventure of the Clapham Cook*, was shown on 8 January 1989. Viewers and critics alike were struck at the amount of hard work that had quite obviously gone into realising the project. For those purists who had longed for an authentic interpretation of the legendary little sleuth, Peter Tory of the *Daily Express* summarised the general view when he wrote in his column on 21 January: 'Quite simply, Mr. Suchet's performance as Poirot must be exactly as Miss Christie imagined him.'

Midway through that first season – which achieved viewing figures averaging 12 million per episode – *The Listener* reinforced Peter Tory's

David Suchet receives a rare kiss in *The Veiled Lady*.

Poirot's mixture of self-importance and teasing demonstrated by David Suchet.

Opposite:
Costume design has been an outstanding feature of the series.

verdict. 'David Suchet's Hercule Poirot is the most pleasing and 'authentic' piece of fabrication ... His character is almost as meticulously thought-out as Jeremy Brett's Sherlock Holmes. Suchet also brings out Poirot's self-importance, but flavours it with a touch of teasing.'

A number of newspapers and TV magazines also received letters from readers about the series: an 'avid Agatha Christie fan', L. Smith from Worcestershire being one of many who wrote to *TV Guide* at the end of the series in April offering his congratulations to LWT and all those involved for their 'brilliant production'. He added, 'I was especially impressed with the wonderful David Suchet as for the first time the Belgian detective has been presented exactly how he was depicted in Agatha Christie's work'.

Six years later, the Poirot bandwagon runs on unchecked. In the interim it has won four BAFTA Awards, including those for costume design, make-up and graphics, and is now being shown in fifty-one countries, including America, Canada, Australia, Japan, France, Germany, Spain and Scandinavia. Curiously, though, Poirot's worldwide appeal has still to find an audience in his home country, Belgium.

It has also become LWT's top-selling drama series, and to coincide with the showing of two more two-hour specials in the autumn of 1995 – *Dumb Witness* and *Murder on the Links* – a whole new range of associated souvenirs are being launched, including videos, scale models of the Thirties cars used in the series and a medallion bearing the head of the famous detective.

The striking success of Poirot in America has been helped by David Suchet visiting the country on a promotion tour – though he did draw the line at appearing in costume.

'I'm always happy to talk about the character,' David told his hosts, 'but I am not prepared to dress up as Poirot outside the studios.'

On the other hand, his visit did confirm his long-held distaste for many American TV crime series, which he says are too fast, noisy and violent – a view he believes Poirot would share.

'Poirot is not violent man. I think he's a secret sensualist, who likes nice things to look at and likes good food. A lot of Americans do think he is a bit old-fashioned, but I believe that is a big point in his favour. He is old-fashioned – and courteous. Obviously there are a lot of people there who enjoy the series, and I like to think the little phrase I coined to explain the show to journalists helped – Poirot is *Upstairs,*

Poirot searching for another clue in an unlikely situation.

Downstairs with clues!'

This is obviously too simplistic an explanation for a television phenomenon which one newspaper has claimed is watched by 700 million people world wide. Perhaps the one person in the best position to give a reason is the man for whom Poirot has become a dream-turned-realisation – producer Brian Eastman.

'I believe it is very largely due to Agatha Christie's writing,' he says, with barely a moment for reflection. 'She was the prime exponent of what you might call the 'Jigsaw Theory' of detective novels. That is, she would spend the first two thirds of the novel laying out in front of the reader a whole series of jigsaw pieces. And as she did so, the reader might think, 'I wonder how this fits together?' And as he went along he would be trying to fit it all together. Then in the last third of the book she would fit it all together and the reader would kick himself for having joined the wrong bits to one another. But there would still be the delight at seeing it all fitted together.

'That is a very, very clever form of entertainment. And it's what it all comes down to whether you are reading a book or watching television. Sit an audience down, show them a series of jigsaw pieces, tempt them into piecing them together, and then show them how it is *really* done. That's what her books are and that is what our films are – and there is just something very instinctive in the human brain that responds to that kind of storytelling.'

Brian sits back in his chair for a moment, as if the past decade of his life is suddenly flashing across his mind. Then he continues with the certainty of someone who has earned his success.

'What we have managed to do, I think, is to take what Agatha wrote and make it work very well on television. I believe it all comes down to that very fundamental kind of storytelling — we couldn't have achieved anything without it. What we have brought to it is a wonderful actor playing the storyteller — so to speak — the man who is going to put all the jigsaw pieces together for you and does it terribly well. We have also rooted the series in a period of time and featured a form of design and architecture which people have found extremely interesting. That is what we have added to the jigsaw.'

The popularity of Poirot has brought Brian a mixture of pride and amazement. Pride at having satisfied the demands of Agatha Christie's understandably demanding executors, and the amazement at the icon which the suave, brainy and egotistical detective has now become. He cites a typical example.

'It is rather flattering for us constantly to see references in the press to pieces of Bauhaus furniture and Thirties architecture as being 'Poirot furnishings' or 'Poirot buildings'. In a way, I feel a bit ashamed about it, because they are talking about the work of some of the great designers and architects of this century whose work has filtered through all our lives in many different ways. Certainly, those buildings of the Thirties were a bit of an oddity and have been largely ignored. We just happen to have brought them to the fore again. Then all of a sudden I hear someone talking about Lubetkin or one of the other great designers of that period and referring to their work as 'Poirot buildings'.

'I am pleased if more attention is given to this form of architecture as a result of our series,' Brian says by way of the last word. 'Poirot gives himself enough praise for a lot of things without taking the credit for *that* as well!'

THE LABOURS OF HERCULE

The dapper little man walking with such precise steps along the gravel driveway of the old mansion house in the bright morning sunshine was somehow familiar. It was something about the shape of his head, the curl of his moustache and the clothes he was wearing that at once evoked memories. But what was this immaculately-dressed, town dweller doing in the heart of the countryside on such a day? And surely his figure was leaner, the face younger, and, when he lifted his bowler hat in greeting, the hair somewhat thicker?

It was the casually dressed television film crew in their jeans, sweaters and T- shirts on one of the neatly manicured lawns beside the driveway that confirmed the suspicion. For this was, in fact, the major outside location for *The Mysterious Affair at Styles* – a new adaptation of Agatha's novel which had introduced Hercule Poirot to readers. On a July morning in 1990 it was being filmed as a two-hour TV special to mark the authoress' centenary that autumn.

The figure with the neat walk and twinkling eyes was, of course, David Suchet, already familiar to millions of television viewers thanks to two very successful series of Poirot, and now on his way from make-up to film a scene from the novel that had set the whole remarkable legend in motion. The dark grey suit was as freshly pressed and free from a speck of dirt as ever. The neck-tie fastened under his wing-collar by a silver ring was exactly positioned; while a watch and chain hung across his waistcoat glinting in the sunshine. In his right hand the actor carried the familiar walking stick, and in the left a rather less-familiar brown leather briefcase.

What was altogether different about this episode of Poirot from those which had gone before was that the little detective was now a younger man. A man, in fact, who had only just arrived in England to

escape from the carnage of the First World War that had driven him and seven fellow countrymen from their homes in Belgium to find refuge in Styles St Mary, courtesy of the owner of Styles Court. Missing now from David Suchet's usual make-up was the padding that made him appear shorter and more rounded, while his head was partially covered with a new hairpiece to make the immaculately groomed hair look thicker. His moustache was, though, as meticulously manicured as ever – evidence, if such was needed, that fastidiousness was not something that had come late to Hercule Poirot or would be allowed to lessen in his new surroundings.

'It eez certainly a change not to 'ave to wear all ze padding on an 'ot day like today,' David says with a wink, 'and ze whig is made specially so zat I look a leetle less bald than usual. But I am not long in England, so my English she is not so good. *N'est-ce pas?'*

The way in which David slips into the subtle accent he has perfected

On location for *The Mysterious Affair at Styles* – director Ross Devenish with David Suchet.

Poirot with his briefcase, containing the 'tools of his profession'.

for his character the moment he puts on his costume is just one of the many surprises to be experienced at first hand on a day such as this. In fact, he retains the voice effortlessly throughout the morning and afternoon when speaking on camera or else while waiting for the next take. So totally has David immersed himself in the role that he says he even finds himself *thinking* like Poirot when he is filming.

Another surprise that July morning was the location of the shoot. Although Agatha Christie was rarely specific about the settings of her stories, in the case of *The Mysterious Affair at Styles* she made this quite clear right at the very beginning of the story. In Chapter One she had informed readers that the events surrounding the murder of Mrs Emily Inglethorpe had begun on 5 July at the wealthy lady's mansion, Styles Court, in the village of Styles St Mary, Essex.

The day itself was almost exactly right – but the reconstruction of events actually took place over 100 miles away from rural Essex at Chavenage House in Horsley, Gloucestershire.

Set in the heart of the Cotswolds, Chavenage is, however, remarkably similar in layout to that of Styles Court.

When first seen through the tall gatepiers which guard the driveway to the circular forecourt, the house with its golden stone walls and lichened grey roofs well deserves its description of 'a perfect example of a Cotswold manor house'. Indeed, in a feature article about the property in *Country Life* in April 1911 – just a few years before the events at Styles Court – the magazine reported, 'Chavenage is a most liveable and dignified home, retaining in a very marked manner the full flavour of old English country life.'

Some of the most crucial scenes in the TV adaptation were filmed in and around Chavenage, including the day when Poirot is first brought to the mansion by Captain Hastings to start his enquiries into Mrs Inglethorp's sudden death the previous night.

Preparation work had gone on almost since dawn setting up the

16mm camera and sound equipment just beyond the gatepiers to the driveway. Director Ross Devenish and his First Assistant Director, Simon Hinkly, had been in consultation about camera positions and sound levels with Director of Photography Vernon Layton, Camera Operator Stephen Alcorn and Sound Recordist Ken Weston, for some time before the two principal actors were called.

Just as Poirot had been made younger, so the years had been lifted from the shoulders of Hastings. The Captain is at Styles Court recouperating from war injuries when he unexpectedly finds his old friend living in the village and seeks his help to solve the mystery. Although first seen in his military uniform, for the scenes in question Hastings is more familiarly dressed in a light brown suit and felt trilby hat.

David Suchet and Hugh Fraser find their marks on the driveway and David almost instinctively takes a more precise grip on the leather briefcase in his left hand. It is a prop not often seen in the series, containing the tools of his profession: tweezers, a magnifying glass, a pair of scissors, some test tubes, a syringe and a selection of envelopes into which he can place items of evidence. When the crew are all in their places and a hush of silence has fallen across the mansion and its grounds, Ross Devenish calls for action.

Another location shot of *The Mysterious Affair at Styles.*

The camera's tracking shot takes in the grandeur of Chavenage (aka Styles) as well as focusing on the drama which has recently occurred within. A grey, horse-drawn van with a Red Cross symbol on its side is driven away from the porch by two girls in VAD uniforms. It is carrying the body of Mrs Inglethorp to the mortuary. As it swings down the drive past the two actors, Poirot and Hastings respectfully remove their hats.

The detective is questioning his friend about events in the house the previous night. How much the dead woman had eaten at dinner and how long a period had then elapsed before she had been found suffering her final agonies. When Hastings tells him she ate virtually nothing and over nine hours passed before her death, the detective is understandably puzzled. 'It is,' he says, 'one of those curiously leetle facts, *mon ami.*'

David pauses just a beat. 'We put it *here*,' he adds and touches the side of his forehead with his right forefinger. . .

'The Styles Case' – as it is described in the novel – and 'the world-wide notoriety which attended it', also marks the start of the famous detective partnership between Poirot and Hastings, which was destined to become one of the best-known in literature. And it was this element of the story, as well as the solving of the murder, that Ross Devenish was anxious to bring to the screen.

'Although viewers of the series had already seen Poirot and Hastings at work, it was at Styles that the partnership really began,' explains Ross, a veteran of several classic period TV adaptations including *Bleak House*, *Happy Valley* and *Death of a Son*. 'So we wanted to try and show how this started and what it was that enabled them to get on so well together considering their very different backgrounds and temperaments. Agatha Christie actually wrote the original book more carefully than some of the later ones when she had become disillusioned with Poirot, and the Poirot-Hastings partnership is described more delicately than one might expect from its later treatment. Poirot is, in fact, given a lot more depth and is not such a figure of eccentricities

The meeting of two friends which starts a career of detection.

and catch-phrases, while Hastings is not a caricature.

'Hastings was certainly not the buffoon he is sometimes suggested to be, and although Poirot is vain he is also too clever a person to want to waste his time on someone who doesn't have special qualities of their own. They do make a good team – although it is a team of which Poirot is most definitely the senior partner!'

Once everything was in place shooting could begin. Still, it was only when Ray Cooper, the clapper/loader, snapped together his digital clapperboard that all the months of planning which had begun the previous year with Clive Exton's script outline that the project at last started to become a reality. (Interestingly, although most people are familiar with the concept of the clapperboard, few outside the industry are aware that its real purpose is to enable the editor of the film to synchronise the picture and sound. By finding the first frame on the film where the clapperboard is completely closed and the exact point on the soundtrack where the 'snap' of the board is first heard, he can make sure that sound and picture run together and the actors are not speaking 'out of sync'.

Those who worked on *The Mysterious Affair at Styles* remember it as a happy shoot. Apart from the major location work at Chavenage, a

David Suchet and Hugh Fraser share a thoughtful moment during filming.

The clapperboard — seen on every shot, but never on screen.

number of scenes were also filmed at Twickenham Studios, while two days were spent at another stylish old Tudor mansion, Chenies Manor House, which is situated near Amersham in the shadow of the Chiltern Hills. This imposing building, with its red-brick walls and mullioned windows, famous for its tall, twisting chimneys, was for many years the home of the Russells, the Dukes of Bedford. Several interior shots were filmed here: all ostensibly in rooms that were supposed to be part of Styles Court — thereby turning a little piece of Buckinghamshire into faraway Essex, too!

When *The Mysterious Affair at Styles* was screened the day after hundredth anniversary of Agatha's birth on Sunday, 16 September 1990, the audience figures confirmed that the Poirot series now had a real grip on the nation's imagination. Rachel Harland of the *Daily Mirror* echoed what both viewers and readers undoubtedly felt: 'Our old friend Poirot is wearing well as he helped celebrate Agatha Christie's 100th anniversary.'

Whether the authoress had ever imagined that her anniversary might have been celebrated with an adaptation of this story is impossible to guess, but she can certainly never have believed when she originally wrote the novel in 1916 that the little Belgian sleuth would ultimately become such an archetypal figure. In fact, when the manuscript was rejected by six London publishers and was then held for more than eighteen months at John Lane before finally being accepted for publication in 1920, the young authoress might have wondered whether he had any future at all! (Perhaps she even subconsciously nursed such reservations, because she suggested to Lane that the book might appear under a pseudonym such as Mostyn Grey or Martin West; thankfully they dissuaded her.)

Agatha Christie's life has been detailed in her own autobiography and several other studies of her work, but some facts relevant to the creation of Poirot are, I think, deserving of mention here. Agatha Mary Clarissa Miller was born on 15 September, 1890, at Ashfield, the family home in Torquay, Devon. She was the youngest child of a wealthy American expatriate, Frederick Alvah Miller and his English wife, Clarissa. When her father died suddenly in 1901, however, Agatha and the other members of her family were left in rather reduced circumstances, and she was educated at home by her mother. She did, though, go to a finishing school in Paris in 1906 where she revealed a talent as a singer and pianist.

Back in Torquay she lead a busy social life, eventually meeting and marrying Lieutenant (later Colonel) Archibald Christie of the Royal Field Artillery in 1914. (They were divorced in 1928 and she later married the archaeologist, Sir Max Mallowan.) It was at this period of Agatha's life that the seeds of her talent as a writer of crime fiction were sown. Because the young couple were separated for long periods due to the war, Agatha filled in her time by joining the VADs (Volunteer Aid Detachment) in Torquay, where she initially worked on the wards of Torbay Hospital before becoming a pharmaceutical dispenser. This was to provide her with an extensive knowledge of the power of chemicals and poisons – in particular curare, arsenic and digitalis – which would later prove so useful in her stories.

According to Agatha, she was first encouraged to write at the age of twenty by her mother when she was confined to bed with the 'flu. A day later, she had finished her first short story, *The House of Beauty*, and though it was never published and she described it as 'amateurishly written', the young woman had taken the first step towards her ultimate career. Two more stories followed, plus a romantic novel which she called *Snow Upon the Desert* – but it was evident to her that she was struggling to find her true metier.

It was during the slack periods at the dispensary in Torquay in 1915 that Agatha once again thought about writing. Her older sister, Madge, had earlier introduced her to crime fiction through a collection of the Sherlock Holmes' cases. Very impressed by them, Agatha had also read one or two other writers in the genre. When she decided to try and write a mystery herself – so the story goes – Madge challenged

Waiting for action – some of the cast and crew filming *The Mysterious Affair at Styles.*

her, 'I'll bet you can't write one in which the reader can't guess the murderer.'

Agatha's work with poisons at once gave her the means for her murder. A family home with undercurrents of jealousy and suspicion provided the setting. But what about the detective?

'A Belgian came into my head – it was a simple as that,' Agatha was once quoted as saying. In her autobiography she was a little more specific.

Who could I have as a detective? I reviewed such detectives as I had met and admired in books. There was Sherlock Holmes, the one and only – I should never be able to emulate him. There was Arsene Lupin – was he a criminal or detective? Anyway, not my kind. There was the young journalist Rouletabille in The Mystery of the Yellow Room – that was the sort of person whom I would like to invent.

Then I remembered our Belgian refugees. We had quite a colony of refugees living in the parish of Tor. Why not make my detective a Belgian, I thought? There were all types of refugees. How about a refugee police officer? A retired police officer. Not too young a one. . .

Agatha added a little more information to this when talking to Godfrey Winn of the *Daily Mail* in September 1970 during one of her rare interviews. He had asked her if there was an actual prototype for Poirot.

'No, he was entirely imaginary,' she answered the journalist. 'As my father was American I might just as easily have given my detective a transatlantic flavour, but I settled for a Belgian instead. You know, I made such a stupid mistake in the beginning over Poirot? I wrote that he had already retired from the Belgian equivalent of Scotland Yard which makes him so terrible old today. In fact, my age!'

Mistake or not, the Poirot who emerged in the pages of *The Mysterious Affair at Styles* – the 'trained detective' with his admiration for Sherlock Holmes and ability to apply 'the little grey cells of the brain' to solving crime – caught the attention of readers and critics alike. *The Times Literary Supplement*, not generally given to noticing first novels, was the first periodical to mention the book in what was, quite simply, a rave review published on 2 March, 1921.

'The only fault in this brilliant story,' the anonymous reviewer began, 'is that it is almost too ingenious. Styles is a country house in Essex and the mysterious affair is the death of its mistress by poison. There is an

Opposite:
Agatha Christie

extraordinary assortment of persons in the house and the neighbour-hood, and suspicion is tossed about from one to another among them in the most baffling way. But the problem does not baffle little M Poirot, a retired Belgian detective, who is one of the queer characters brought together at Styles, and after many singular twists and turns he lays his hand on the guilty persons. They are superhumanly clever, but he is cleverer still. It is said to be the author's first book, and the result of a bet about the possibility of writing a detective story in which the reader would not be able to spot the criminal. Every reader must admit that the bet was won'.

Delighted as she must have been by that verdict, Agatha was even more pleased by the fact that the *Pharmaceutical Journal* not only reviewed the book but complemented her on her professionalism. 'This detective story deals with poisons in a knowledgeable way, and not with the nonsense about untraceable substances that so often happens. Miss Agatha Christie knows her job.'

That was to be the start of the legend which over the next fifty-five would result in the thirty-three novels and fifty-six short stories about Hercule Poirot – which in their turn generated the innumerable plays, films, radio adaptations and TV versions of the little sleuth's cases.

There has, of course, been much debate among some students of Agatha Christie's work as to whether Poirot did indeed just slip into her mind or whether he might have been influenced by earlier detective stories she had read. Certainly before he appeared in print G.K.Chesterton had give readers his Hercule Flameau; an American authoress, Marie Bellow Lowndes, had written several cases about a French detective named Hercule Popeau; and in 1909, an English publication, *The New Magazine*, had run a serial by Frank Howell Evans about a retired French police officer Jules Poiret, nicknamed 'Old Pawray', who lived in England and took on seemingly impossible cases from the comfort of his London flat.

A real-life original has also been suggested in Ignatius Pollaky, a famous Austro-Hungarian detective, who came to England and in 1861 set up his own Continental Inquiry Service in Paddington, London. Pollaky apparently wore a splendid waxed moustache like Poirot, and drew much of his skill in catching criminals from a remark-able insight into human characteristics. He died in retirement in 1918.

Arguments about whether or not Agatha knew of Pollaky or had read any of the cases of the fictional detectives are the stuff of contro-versy and like her own mysteries will no doubt continue to engage the interest of researchers for years to come. All she *is* on record as saying is that she chose the Christian name Hercule to make the little detective 'sound and feel important' and Poirot 'because it just seemed suitable' – 'But I hadn't read many detective stories because there weren't very many to read,' she added.

No claims of literary role models or the influence of other writers can, however, diminish in any way the impact of Hercule Poirot who, within a few years of his debut, had undeniably become one of the greatest sleuths of fiction, while all the others I have mentioned were virtually forgotten.

There is, though, no secret about the fact that Agatha, like her mentor, Sir Arthur Conan Doyle with Sherlock Holmes, grew tired of her creation. In 1938 she confided to the *Daily Mail*, 'There are moments when I have felt why – why – *why* did I ever invent this detestable, bombastic, tiresome little creature... eternally twirling his moustache and tilting his egg-shaped head? By a few strokes of the pen I could destroy him utterly.'

But the demands of her publishers and huge readership made any such action out of the question. As she confided to her agent, Hughes Massie, 'Poirot is insufferable – most public men are who have lived too long. But none of them like retiring. So I'm afraid Poirot won't either – certainly not while he is my chief source of income.'

'This tiresome little creature' Agatha Christie once said of Hercule Poirot.

Yet this said, with the advent of the Second World War Agatha took the opportunity during the Blitz when she was living in London once more undertaking voluntary hospital work to finish off the man she had created during the previous conflict. Agatha entitled her manuscript *Curtain: Poirot's Last Case*, and after debating about publishing it gave instructions that it should not be published until after her death. In fact, she relented just three months before this occurred and allowed the typescript – which had been locked away in a fire- and burglar-proof safe throughout the intervening thirty-five years – to appear in October 1975. This change of heart was apparently the result of persuasion by her publisher, Sir William Collins, who convinced Agatha that 'unless Poirot was killed off by her own hand, after her death other writers might try to keep him alive'.

News of Poirot's 'death' actually became public before the novel reached the bookshops. This once again demonstrated what a truly unique figure he was when 'obituaries' about him were printed in all the English newspapers (see a typical example here from the *Daily Telegraph* of 7 August, 1975) and in the front page of the *New York Times* – an accolade afforded to very few 'real' people let alone a

The Daily Telegraph, Thursday, August 7, 1975

DAME AGATHA'S FINAL SOLUTION FOR POIROT

By GODFREY BARKER

M. HERCULE POIROT, the well-known Belgian detective, has died at the home of a friend in Styles St Mary, Essex, his physician, Dr John Franklyn, announced yesterday.

A report certifying the cause of death as coronary thrombosis is due on Sept. 29 from his close friend and inspirer, Dame Agatha Christie.

Other close friends of the moustachioed gastronome maintain, however, that his death occurred through far from natural causes.

But the fact remains that Poirot, who has figured in dozens of the 90-plus mysteries, novels and short stories of Dame Agatha, 85, is now dead and gone.

Rot sets in

From the moment that Poirot hobbles on stage in this epilogue to a great career, "Curtain—or Poirot's Last Case," it is clear the rot has set in.

The jet black of his sleek hair now comes out of a hair-dye bottle; his emaciated frame is supported in a wheel-chair, arthritis grips him.

Twenty four hour nursing is now required to keep the famous "grey cells" in tune. The once besplendent pudgy figure in his mauve silk dressing gown now has to be washed, put to bed, doped with sleeping tablets and dressed in the morning.

"His health's rotten, of course," his doctor declares revealingly outside the bedroom door after another touch of the shudders around Poirot's heart.

For once, the famous remedies do not work. All the coats, mufflers and scarves to protect him from draughts, the Perrier waters to calm the liver, the noxious tisanes for the fluxions poitrines (flu to us) are of no avail.

Poirot is but a shadow of the vigorous dandy who used to demolish two tornados, a delicate cream cheese, coffee and liqueurs at lunch-time, pick locks and clamber into coal lifts if need be, and put his large foot in criminals' front doors throughout North London and the Home Counties.

"Sacré! Sapristi!" and "Mille tonnerres!" he would cry at grease stains on his grey suit, in whose bulging pockets he kept talcum powder, clothes brushes, silk thread for placing across door jambs, a large turnip watch, a whistle, a pocket-book and curling tongs for his moustaches.

He would occasionally "have a go" at the criminal classes, in his younger days.

"Allez!" he cried on one typical occasion as he enveloped the neck of an intruding Italian with a woollen scarf.

Much vaunted brainpower

In his heyday the tri-lingual sleuth who never grasped English, was the greatest international detective of them all, the employee of aristocrats such as Lords Cronshaw, Estair and Yardly and "perfect women" like Miss Esmèe Farquhar though he was not above working for insurance companies if need be.

His much vaunted brainpower was based on close reading of "The Daily Megaphone" and "The Daily Newsmonger." Faded copies of "Society Gossip" littered his coffee table; the "Almanach de Gotha," and Burke's Peerage (which he preferred to Debrett) were in the bedroom.

Signs of decay

Physically fearless, Poirot regarded dead bodies as routine—"it is not pretty" was a typical rejoinder — and was totally unmoved by ghosts, even when they appeared with blood dripping from their fingers in the dark.

An excellent judge of diamonds, a connoisseur of scent, Poirot was "un peu snob" (as the Belgians say) and affected a cane. But his image was occasionally dented when his moustaches fell into the soup.

But the signs of decay were always there. Too much thick, sweet chocolate; too many tiny Russian cigarettes; too many taxis and too little walking; seasickness on his way to Egypt for a cure; disaster on the camels when he arrived.

But lovers of Dame Agatha's novels will be relieved that Miss Marple, her other ace detective, remains in good health, and a mystery will continue to appear every autumn for the future as it has done every year since 1924, according to Collins, her publishers.

Readers can rest assured that the novel, though Poirot's last, is one of Dame Agatha's best. It dates from 1940, in the middle of her vintage period, and has lain in a vault for 35 years.

Editorial comment—P14

figment of the imagination!

The reviews of *Curtain* mixed a sadness at the demise of Poirot with an admiration for Agatha's unequalled ability for plotting. *The Times Literary Supplement*, which had first greeted Poirot's arrival, was as enthusiastic as it had been fifty-five years earlier. The reviewer this time, however, was not anonymous but the distinguished critic Francis Wyndham who wrote, 'The solution, when it is finally sprung, turns out to be as outrageously satisfying as Agatha Christie's best. As she presumably intended, in this story she has brought off the bluff to end them all.'

Curtain also returned full circle by once again being set at Styles Court where Poirot was now a shadow of his former self: a cripple in a wheelchair, cared for by others who had to wash and dress the man who all his life had been so fastidious about his appearance. Even Poirot's moustache and hair, the apogee of his vanity, were now seen to be badly dyed. Other things had also changed in the interim, too.

No longer was Styles Court a family home, but had been converted into a guest house full of small rooms with cramped bathrooms. The building itself was badly in need of a new coat of paint, and while the appearance of the surrounding park was much the same, the sweep of driveway was untidy, with weeds punctuating the gravel. The village of Styles St Mary was almost completely unrecognisable, too, albeit that the railway station was still there to bring Hastings for what would prove his final reunion with Poirot. Now along the main street there were petrol stations, a cinema, two more inns and even a row of council houses.

This novel, which ended the Poirot saga in literary terms, now figures as significantly in Brian Eastman's future plans for the LWT series as did *The Mysterious Affair at Styles*. To date, Carnival Films have produced fifty-six hours of television time and exhausted all the short stories as well as eight novels.

'But we still have twenty-five novels to work on, and David and I want to make them all,' he says enthusiastically. 'Agatha does, of course, age Poirot in the later stories, and eventually we shall come to books that cannot be set pre-war. Those, that is, which have integral parts that can only occur because of post-war activities. So we have been facing up to the fact that we shall have to see him go through the Second World War and then into the Fifties and Sixties. In fact, David is already thinking of how he will allow himself to age bit by bit.

'The last book we'll film will, of course, be *Curtain*. Then, like Agatha Christie, we'll lay the character to rest. But that will be over quite a long period – five to six years I estimate – so there are still a lot more cases of Poirot to come!'

THE SECRET OF WHITEHAVEN MANSIONS

Secluded Charterhouse Square lies in the shadow of ancient St Bartholomew's Medical school and just a stone's throw from the oblong mass of the old Smithfield Market buildings. It is one of London's last private gated garden squares to which its residents have keys, and is surrounded on all sides by buildings which bear silent witness to its long history. To walk into it from the endless traffic on Clerkenwell Road or the busy commercial streets of Holborn is to enter a little haven trapped in a time warp.

There is, in fact, a peacefulness about the place with its cobbled roadway, mix of architectural styles and swathe of tree-lined lawns that makes it seem anywhere but in the heart of a great city. Small wonder that the novelist William Makepeace Thackeray who studied here in 1822 at the famous Charterhouse School before it was transferred to Godalming, Surrey, should have written wistfully some years later of its 'blackened trees and garden, surrounded by ancient houses now slumbering like pensioners in the sunshine.' Little has changed in the intervening 170 years.

It is in this square that the makers of Poirot have worked another of their remarkable examples of illusion. For the flat from which the little detective conducts his business is not to be found in Mayfair – as described in the original books – but by courtesy of the television eye on the northern side of Charterhouse Square. Or to be more precise the outside of the mansion where he lives, which stands there in the everyday guise of Florin Court.

Readers familiar with Agatha's works will recall that Poirot first set up as a private enquiry agent at 14, Farraway Street in London, where he shared accommodation with Captain Hastings. Then after Hastings' marriage and departure for the Argentine, he moved to a new apart-

Opposite:
David Suchet on location outside Florin Court in Charterhouse Square.

'One of the newest type of service flats in London'. Whitehaven Mansions as seen in the LWT series.

ment. This Hastings describes on his return to England with typical brevity in *The ABC Murders* (1936):

> *I found him installed in one of the newest type of service flats in London. I accused him (and he admitted the fact) of having chosen this particular building entirely on account of its strictly geometrical appearance and proportions.*
>
> *'But yes, my friend, it is of a most pleasing symmetry, do you not find it so?'*

There seems no reason to doubt that Poirot would have looked for his new address with all the meticulous care for which he was famous: and in finding somewhere to double for the flat, Brian Eastman and his team have been equally painstaking. Interestingly, the name of Poirot's block of flats – which crime historian H.R.F. Keating has described as 'a paragon of parellelisms' – is alternately described by Agatha in the later Poirot cases as Whitehaven Mansions, Whitehouse Mansions and even Whitefriar Mansions. For the TV series, however, Whitehaven Mansions received everyone's approval.

Brian explains how this particularly faithful stand-in with its geometrical appearance and proportions which would certainly have satisfied the Belgian detective's passion for order and method was discovered.

'Actually there are lots of fine Thirties buildings in London,' he says. 'And once we had decided to make modern-Thirties architecture a feature of the stories, we set out to compile a list of all the buildings from that era that were available within striking distance of central London. Since then we've woven a lot of them into the films.

'We had two or three places that we *could* have used as Poirot's apartment – but there were several reasons that finally made us decide on Florin Court. In the books Poirot is described as living in 'a Mayfair square'. But the interesting thing about Charterhouse is that nobody ever thinks it is in the city of London – Although you can believe it *looks* like Mayfair – which is what makes it unusual.

'We were also very lucky that the property developers who had recently bought Florin Court had just completely refurbished it, putting the exterior back to its original pristine condition. So from the photographic point of view we had this lovely element of a clean, new building set between two nineteenth-century properties. So right from the opening shot we were establishing the point of the series.'

The renovations to Florin Court had been completed at a cost of £2 million and the eighty-four flats were ready for occupation in the summer of 1988 when the Poirot team came across it during their search for Poirot's apartment.

'It was just what we wanted,' Brian Eastman recalls. 'And the developers agreed to let us film the building almost before they had let any of the apartments at all. So we got permission to close off the whole area for one weekend and set up our cameras. We shot continuously for a seventy-two-hour period – all through one day, then through the night, and all the next day. We knew it was important to do this because we would never be able to come back and find everything the same.

'Obviously once the apartments were let there would be different sorts of curtains hanging at the windows. Things like that would change all the time and it would be impossible for us to match up everything. So we filmed Florin Court from every angle and in every kind of light and darkness. We were not shooting material specifically for the first series, but to build up a library of general footage that we could weave into the stories any time we wanted. In fact, we have been able to use the shots we made that weekend right up to the present day. And we'll probably go on using them well into the future.'

Brian says that the team have, however, made a few brief return visits to Charterhouse Square to film 'Whitehaven Mansions' – but only during daylight hours. As he rightly guessed, the windows are now hung with a variety of chintz curtains, with potted plants and exotic flowers much in evidence. On these occasions, though, in an amusing twist of fate, it has been the camera crew who have found themselves under scrutiny from the building – not by the occupants, but rather the closed-circuit TV which monitors everyone entering and leaving Florin

Court. It is a security system of which Poirot would undoubtedly approve.

'There has been the odd occasion when we've needed some extra footage,' says Brian, 'such as a scene in front of the entrance or maybe in one of the streets nearby. Thankfully the square is still as easy and quiet and as much in the period as ever. But mostly we rely on the footage that we shot all those years ago to cut in with new material.'

Although, courtesy of this footage, establishing shots of Poirot and Hastings at Whitehaven Mansions can be inserted at any time, when they reappear on camera in the detective's meticulous flat *inside* the building they are actually anything up to ten miles away in Twickenham, or perhaps even Pinewood or Elstree. For this is the second intriguing secret in the story of the Poirot locations...

The sensation of entering another time warp is also felt by the visitor to the set of Poirot's flat when it is erected in Twickenham Film Studios. For here the same careful attention to detail has been brought to bear in the creation of an environment that not only matches the Florin Court exterior, but is in keeping with Agatha's admittedly scant descriptions of the actual room in her stories, and not least of all in paying strict attention to her character's obsession with order.

Although Brian and his team combed London to find many of the buildings which appear in the series, they never for a moment imagined that the little detective's flat could be anything other than a set – and one that would have to be durable if, as they hoped, the series became long-running.

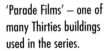

'Parade Films' – one of many Thirties buildings used in the series.

On the Poirot set in
Twickenham studios.

'We built Poirot's apartment as a set for Series One and we have
used it ever since,' Brian explains. 'There have been the occasional
modifications, but basically it is the same one all the time to achieve the
sense of continuity. It is taken down after each series and then reassem-
bled for the next. For the first five years it was filmed entirely at
Twickenham Studios, but we have also been to Pinewood.

'In fact, the decision now where to erect the set rather depends on
where the main locations for the next series are going to be. If they are
south of London, then we'll use Twickenham. But if they are to the west
then maybe we'll go to Pinewood, while if we have to go north then
Elstree could well be the place. Because filming is such a time consum-
ing and expensive business, we do this to keep everyone's travelling
time to a minimum.'

Twickenham, however, remains the studio most associated with the
series, and apart from the fact that Poirot's flat has been shot there
more times than anywhere else, there are also a number of unspoiled
Thirties buildings in the vicinity which have been commandeered for
location filming.

'The style we went in for was austere: rather bleak and Germanic,'
recalls Mike who learned his craft as a designer of period television
while working on *Upstairs, Downstairs*, the Seventies LWT series about
life in a London house between 1910 and 1930. 'It was not all Art
Deco, though, which is what most people think the Thirties is all about.
By putting the series into the year 1936, I believe we gave it a strong
visual identity.

'At the time, this new style was called the Modern Movement – but it was a style that never really caught on in Britain. Yet Poirot was bang up to date, and in the very first series we tried to show how 'modern' the Thirties were. Even though the war was not far away, it was still an era when cruise liners and cocktails proliferated, and if you had the money life was really rather pleasant.'

Finding the props which have made this set so authentic was the task of Art Director Caroline Smith, who initially directed her attentions towards literary and pictorial sources.

'I started by scouring old magazines and books,' she recalls. 'It was great fun studying all the old Thirties photographs and illustrations because it was such a stylish period. I particularly love all that Art Deco furniture.'

Virtually everything on the set from the sunken armchairs and narrow tables to the smallest light fittings and ornate decorations have been hired from a prop company.

'Sometimes I like to buy props,' says Caroline, 'but unfortunately the prices have just rocketed in recent years. However, we did manage to get a 'fountain' light for Poirot's dining-room table that cost us £150 at auction, and an Art Deco desk lamp that cost £70. Most things, though, we have to hire.'

A smile crosses her face. 'I expect some keen-eyed viewers of the series may think they have seen something in Poirot that looks rather familiar. Well, I have to admit that you do sometimes see pieces that have cropped up in other series!'

The costumes which the actors and actresses wear are also either faithful reproductions or originals. One of the most striking examples of this is the blue pinstripe suit regularly worn by Hugh Fraser, which he jokingly refers to as being 'older than I am and certainly much better looked-after!'

The same precise attention is also evident in make-up, where the first make-up supervisor, Hilary Martin, set the standards for the series.

'Getting the correct look for the period was essential or else all the other hard work could have been undone,' says Hilary. 'I did quite a lot of research, looking through old copies of *Vogue* in particular, so that I'd get it exactly right. Women then were beginning to grow their hair again after the bobs of the Twenties, and their make-up was very matt, with lots of powder. They used a

Hugh Fraser in his trade-mark blue pinstripe suit with David Suchet and Hermione Norris.

narrow colour range and liked to look very pale with heavy emphasis on the lips and eyebrows.'

The work of this behind-the-scenes quartet, Mike, Rob, Caroline and Hilary undoubtedly played an important part in creating the Thirties feel of Poirot's flat as well as the authentic period look of David Suchet and his co-stars. Indeed, the success of the series has lead to LWT receiving a considerable number of letters from viewers asking for information on how to copy what they have seen on the screen.

'It wouldn't be difficult to recreate the Poirot style in your own home,' Mike Oxley believes. 'There is plenty of good repro furniture about, and the basic feel is of space and symmetry. In the thirties people were taking risks with design and that is what makes it exciting, even today.'

Thirties make-up as worn by Bridget Forsythe in *The Adventure of the Clapham Cook.*

Although the interior and frontage of the little detective's flat are the two most constant images in Poirot, the production team have used a whole variety of locations as well as specially constructed sets all through the duration of the series. Brian Eastman explains:

'All the films are a mixture of authentic buildings and artificial sets. For the exteriors we mostly need a location. But for the interiors, although we occasionally shoot them in Thirties buildings, more often than not we make the rooms or offices to our own specifications.'

'In fact, building your own set can often be better than trying to find somewhere that already exists. Especially because of the fact that although the outside of quite a few buildings of the period have survived, the interiors more often than not have been changed out of all recognition. So by doing it ourselves we can create a more interesting environment. We find that the slight artificiality of being in the studios is also good for the show and is in keeping with its tone. I think that we probably do more studio work that most other series.'

Aside from Poirot's flat, there is actually only one other location that occurs with any kind of frequency – Chief Inspector Japp's office. This, though, has been cut back to its most basic element, as Brian explains with a wry smile.

'As far as we are concerned,' he says, 'the only thing that we consider constitutes Japp's office is his fan. We have now filmed his office in dozens of different locations. We just put a *fan* down on a

Inspector Japp (Philip Jackson) complete with his ever-present fan.

desk and shoot it – and there you have Japp's office! I suspect, though, that if an eagle-eyed viewer were to put together all the scenes of Japp's office he would probably think, 'Good heavens, this man moves office more than anyone else in the world!' But the fact remains that we can create the right atmosphere with only this wonderful fan!'

It is obviously impossible to catalogue in a book such as this all the places which the series has utilised as settings, and a few typical examples must therefore suffice as a guide to a much bigger total. All, though, have contribute in their own way towards bringing the era of the Thirties alive on the screen and creating the unique visual style of Poirot.

London and its surrounding districts have, naturally, provided by far the greatest number of locations. One of the earliest examples of a building doubling for somewhere completely different occurred in the story of *The Lost Mine* in Series One. This drama focused on the murder of an old Chinaman who had travelled to London to negotiate the sale of some documents about the location of an abandoned mine in Burma believed to still hold rich deposits of ore.

Several crucial scenes concerning this transaction took place in the fictional London and Shanghai Bank, and to represent these premises the production team went into the suburbs to use the Dagenham Civic Centre in Essex. Built in 1932, the Centre is considered a very good example of the architecture of the period, and the frontage has remained largely unchanged in the intervening years.

Edward Bennett, who directed the scenes at the bank featuring David Suchet and co-star, Anthony Bate, commented after the weekend-long shoot, 'We wanted an authentic look, and the Civic Centre is in very good condition. The interiors which we used were just what we needed and very official looking, too. The council offices made for plush banker's rooms and the whole effect was Thirties to a tee.'

For the same story, the production team also went into Bethnal Green, transforming two streets, Columbia Road and Ezra Street, into a striking replica of London's Chinatown in 1936. Because the original Chinatown in Limehouse has long since disappeared, the cobbled streets and period terraced houses of this part of East London proved ideal for the sequence. Vincent Wong and Hugh Fraser were the main actors in the scenes – which Hugh remembers vividly.

'We filmed at night, and the artificial lights gave the whole area a really sinister appearance,' he recalls. 'But what I didn't know until afterwards was that the location had been used before. It was the same street where Mick Jagger and David Bowie had filmed that spectacular video, 'Dancing in the Street'. It was a bit of a contrast to our spot of mayhem supposedly happening in Chinatown!'

An equally surprising change had to be effected in Kent to the Dover Harbour Board offices on the seafront, when the Poirot team changed its appearance to resemble a hotel for the episode of *The Kidnapped Prime Minister*. The story concerned the dramatic disappearance of the PM in the direction of Paris on the eve of a crucial conference, and for this the mercantile offices became the Sea View Hotel. Two other scenes were also filmed in Dover at the Western Park and at St Margaret's.

Another seaside location, Salcombe in Devon, was cheekily dressed

Bethnal Green transformed into London's Chinatown for *The Lost Mine.*

up as a Cornish holiday spot in the first of the two-hour, feature-length specials, *Peril at End House*, which was shown in January 1990. Based on Agatha's 1932 novel – which had been adapted as a play in 1940 by Arthur Ridley and starred Francis L.Sullivan (see 'The Many Faces of Poirot') – the case developed after the arrival of Poirot and Hastings at the Hotel Majestic at St Loo, the 'Queen of Watering Places'. There the pair became embroiled in a murder threat to pretty Nick Buckley (played by Polly Walker), the last of her line, who lived in the isolated End House across the bay.

Instead of using the Cornish Rivièra where the events occur, the eighty-strong production crew and cast descended on old-world Salcombe – long established as a favourite haven for yachtsmen, with one of the West Country's finest natural harbours – for a week of intensive filming. Explained the director, Renny Rye: 'Salcombe actually had more Thirties elements about it than we could find on the Cornish coast – which was our main criterion. A little deception is an essential thing in television, I believe, and as Agatha Christie didn't set her story in any specific Cornish town I hope we didn't upset anyone too much!'

A little Somerset town, Dunster, was also used to double as the Cornish village of Polgar in *The Cornish Mystery*. Once again the production crew had to work a transformation on the picturesque little community, with its famous castle and ancient yarn market. The high street was closed off for a weekend, the numerous gift shops camouflaged and all modern signs removed. Lace curtains were even specially hung in the windows of several shops to create the illusion of private houses.

Dunster in Somerset becomes Polgar in Cornwall for *The Cornish Mystery*.

Turning the clock back sixty years was further achieved by taking down TV aerials, removing the yellow lines on the roadway, and covering the street lights on the side of buildings with heavy-duty masking tape and painting them to blend in with each house. Off-duty policemen were hired to direct traffic through the castle grounds or around Dunster, while shopkeepers in the high street were compensated for the loss of a day's takings. In addition, forty local people found themselves work as extras for the crowd scenes.

The shoot proved a memorable one for the people of Dunster as well as David Suchet.

'It was such a friendly place, and generally unspoiled,' he recalls 'But it looked marvellous without the road markings and all those other trappings of modern life. What a pity that places like that can't be kept that way all the time. There's a lot to be said for the way this country looked in the Thirties.'

Perhaps, though, the cleverest illusion of all was created for one of the most recent episodes, the two-hour long *Hercule Poirot's Christmas* screened on 1 January 1995. For this story, in which the little detective was called away from his quiet Christmas to join the aged misanthrope Simeon Lee (Vernon Dobtcheff) at his snow bound mansion, Gorston

Hall, and there found himself at the centre of a murder mystery plus the theft of some valuable diamonds, was actually filmed during the previous *April*!

Turning spring into winter was the task of Rob Harris who, with a nice touch of humour, chose the little village of Chilham six miles from Canterbury in Kent for his location. The charming village stands on the old Pilgrims' Way to the shrine of Thomas Becket – a fact which is reflected in the mixture of timber, brick and tile houses, shops and inns which line the main street. A square of half-timbered houses lies between the churchyard and the gates of the Norman castle and a redbrick Jacobean mansion, constructed in 1616 for Sir Dudley Digges, a high official in the court of James I. It was on this area that Rob focused his attention for the shoot.

'Apart from turning the clock back to 1936, we also had to change the weather to the middle of winter,' he recalls. 'So once we had removed all the evidence of Nineties England – such as road signs, TV aerials and yellow lines – not to mention dressing the shop windows and fitting out a group of locals as period carol singers, we then had to bring on the snow.'

With the real weather giving no sign of any help, Rob solved the problem with shredded paper – and the village square leading to the fictional Gorston Hall became the scene of a most unseasonal blizzard.

'We made the 'snow' from paper and sprayed it over the houses, the people and the cars with a large hose,' Rob recalls. 'When shooting was actually taking place we even had a chap up on a ladder with the unenviable job of producing the effect of falling snow!'

Chilham near Canterbury was used as the location for *Hercule Poirot's Christmas*.

The illusion of Christmas created by the magic of TV special effects for *Hercule Poirot's Christmas.*

But even the best plans can sometimes go awry, as the designer remembers with a rueful grin.

'Unfortunately April lived up to its reputation,' he says. 'And while we were shooting a shower of rain began to fall. There was no alternative but to go on – and gradually the 'snow' turned into a soggy mass. It wasn't much fun for the cast or crew, but happily we managed to get all the necessary shots in the can before we were overwhelmed by the morass of paper!'

The cost of the illusions which have been another cornerstone to the success of Poirot have often been high – and not without discomfort to the behind-the scenes team, as Rob and the rest of his colleagues will readily bear witness. But no one, either working on the series or viewing it, would deny their remarkable authenticity or visual impact.

THE FILE ON POIROT

The actor whose name has now become synonymous with that of one of the world's most famous fictional detectives actually grew up within hailing distance of the home of the only other literary sleuth who might be considered his character's equal. For the first eight years of his life, David Suchet lived in Chiltern Court, Baker Street, where as the whole world knows Sherlock Holmes had his apartment at 221b.

During these formative years David Suchet developed the sense of singlemindedness and dynamism that he brings to his work and that has made his portrayal of the little Belgian sleuth – 'a meticulous study in enigmatic ingenuity' as one critic has called it – so memorable.

Since he first agreed to take on the role, David has carried with him everywhere a 'File on Poirot' – his characteristics, eccentricities, likes and dislikes, to which he constantly refers. The detail is impressive – it even contains the Thirties phone number of Poirot's first flat: Trafalgar 8137. David also possesses a copy of an autobiographical letter purporting to be 'by' the detective, though it was actually written by Agatha Christie in April 1936 for her American publishers. (A copy of this letter is reprinted here.)

Futhermore, when he is working, David is an obsessive list maker to help him in his performance.

'Whenever I take on a role like Poirot, the first thing I do is make two lists,' he explains in his beautifully modulated bass voice that is quite different from the insinuating tones of Poirot. 'These are for the character and me – the similarities between us and the differences. This isn't as dull as it sounds, because the list of adjectives about me is honest – it is a truthful assessment. You have to dig deep into the potential of your own psyche to play a character truthfully. That means knowing yourself and your flaws.

MY AUTOBIOGRAPHY

by Hercule Poirot

I began work as a member of the detective force in Brussels on the Abercrombie Forger Case in 1904 and for many years was proud to be a member of the detective service in my native Belgium. Since the closing year of the war, I have, as you know, been in London, having rooms for some time with mon vieux ami Hastings...

I set up as a private detective in London... In June of last year I installed myself in one of the newest type of service flats in London, called Whitehaven Mansions, which particular building I chose entirely on account of its strictly geometric appearance and proportion...

I have my little prejudices. Anything in the least crooked or disorderly is a torment to me. In my bookcase, I arrange the tallest book at the end; then the next tallest, and so on. My medicine bottles are placed in a neatly graduated row. If your necktie were not correct, I should find it irresistible not to make it straight for you...

Order and method are my gods. For my breakfast, I have only toast which is cut into neat little squares. The eggs – there must be two – they must be identical in size...

I am five feet four inches high. My head, it is egg-shaped and I carry it a little to one side, the left. My eyes, I am told, shine green when I am excited. My boots are neat patent leather, smart and shiny. My stick is embossed with a gold band. My watch is large and keeps the time exactly. My moustache is the finest in all London...

I own I have a certain disdain for tangible evidence. I prefer just to sit here and think – what mon ami Hastings has called 'employing the little grey cells'. I arrange the facts neatly, each in its proper place...

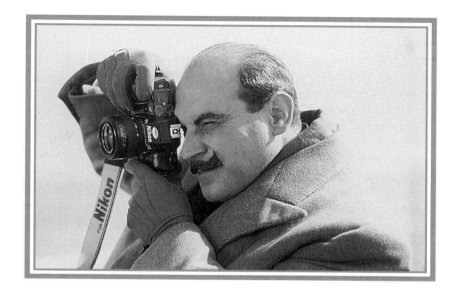

David Suchet is a keen amateur photographer.

'My craft is to become a character, not to bend that character to my personality. If I'm truly to become somebody else than I have to change myself. But I put so much energy into my work that I have none left to play games in real life. This is the real David Suchet, and I've been told that I'm quite boring. For example, I don't like parties, discos, loud music and I'm happily married.

Boring is, however, a totally inappropriate word for a man who has worked with such painstaking attention to detail in order to create a totally believable Poirot.

Although David may change, chamelion-like, from role to role, his own past is fascinating and far from the norm. His name hints at central Europe, and in fact his grandfather on his father's side was from Russia, while his grandmother was German. David explains that in order for his Jewish grandfather to get out of Russia during the *pogroms* he had to change his name to a Russian one for a time before reverting back to Suchet.

If this provides the first hint that David might have been destined for the world of acting, the profession of another of his forebears can be seen as an even clearer indication.

'As a child I was particularly close to my maternal grandfather, James Jerché' he reminices. 'He died when I was eighteen and I didn't feel as if I'd lost a grandfather – I felt as if I'd lost my closest friend. He was a wonderful man, and had been a famous press photographer who got many of the best scoops of the Thirties and Forties. If I mention his name to some of the photographers and cameramen I work with, the older ones go into absolute eulogies about him. He really was a pioneer in his field.'

After eight years living around the corner from Sherlock Holmes, David and the rest of the family – his mother Joan; elder brother, John (today an ITN news presenter); and younger brother, Peter (a top advertising executive) – were moved by their father to Hampstead. Shortly afterwards, David was sent to a boarding school in Kent and then on to Wellington School in Somerset.

Although he says he was homesick for a while, David soon began to enjoy school life.

'I wasn't a very brainy child at school, to be honest,' he continues. 'I was much better at arts and languages than I was at sciences. Before becoming an actor, I had thought about becoming a doctor like my father, which he would have liked, but I didn't have the brains for it. I loved sport as a child, too, although I haven't continued with it, which is a shame. I particularly enjoy cricket, tennis and rugby.'

That David – and his brothers for that matter – should have chosen to go into the media is perhaps not surprising when the evidence of show business in the family blood is brought to light. His maternal grandmother was a song and dance artiste in the music halls, while his mother appeared in a successful musical with Evelyn Laye. She was even signed to appear in a film version of Cleopatra with Merle Oberon, but when the American star had an accident, the film was summarily cancelled.

'A family legend has it that my mother was heartbroken,' says David, 'but her father said to her, 'If you can't take the knocks in this business, you'd better get out'. So she did. It is a piece of advice I've never forgotten.'

Although he had no thoughts of becoming an actor as a child, David did enjoy role playing.

'I always wanted to be a cowboy,' he grins, a twinkle coming into his deep, brown eyes. 'My brother and I had great fights about who was dead and how long it had to be before you could get up again. I was meticulous even then – I always wanted the right gun for the right holster.'

The first time that David acted properly was while he was at Wellington School, and under the most improbable circumstances. 'I was asked to play the part of Mary Bohum in *Richard of Bordeaux*. They actually wanted me to have my legs shaved for the role, but I refused. I said it would have made my rugby socks itch! It never ceases to amaze me how they managed to get a pair of tights in an all-boys school.'

Nonetheless, one of the teachers at Wellington, a Mr Starr, was impressed enough by David's ability to suggest that he audition for the

National Youth Theatre at the Royal Court. Afterwards, as he was watching the scenery men strike a set, he suddenly sensed that this was exactly the sort of atmosphere in which he wanted to spend the rest of his life.

'I announced to my family that I was going to become an actor, and although the news wasn't exactly received with great joy, my parents agreed that as I had already passed my examinations I could go to drama school. Central turned me down flat and said I was no good as an actor, and I did not even turn up for the RADA interview. However, I did go to the one at the London Academy of Dramatic Art, and they offered me a place.'

David soon realised, however, that he was not cut out to be a typical thespian.

'I was the boy that Norman Ayrton, the principal, called to his study and told, 'You know, you really must learn to relax and take off your tie and jacket and wear jeans and T-shirts'. I said, 'But I don't want to wear those things, I'm happy being what I am.' And I suppose I am happy being what I am. I suppose socially I am a conformist in my own sphere, but you won't find me wearing the natural actors' garb of jeans, T-shirt, and a cap. I don't feel comfortable in them.'

It was about this time, too, that he realised that he was not built for playing romantic leads. He was stocky – 5ft 8 inches tall – and had very little hair.

'I realised the image in the mirror was unlikely to make it happen,' he says wrly. 'I saw a balding, bow-legged man who could never really be the next Cary Grant. I didn't need anyone else to tell me. That was

David changes himself
with every part he plays.

my vanity crisis. You see, actors have two choices. They can either change the character of the person they are playing to suit themselves and become a personality player, or you take a risk and change yourself every time according to the part. When I knew I wouldn't be Cary Grant, it allowed me to give everything to the investigation of human nature and to become other people. And ever since I have had such pleasure in doing so.'

David also learned early on to place great store by his voice. 'My voice is one of the last things I would want to lose,' he says earnestly. 'Its a major part of one's personality. I know mine can be very dominating, so sometimes I deliberately lower it.'

After three years of training at LAMDA, David got a position in 1969 as Assistant Stage Manager with the Gateway Theatre in Chester, and there began a gruelling schedule of a different play every ten days. He remembers his first starring role with a little shudder. He was asked to play Shylock, and at twenty-three was probably one of the youngest actors to have undertaken the demanding part.

'I remember thinking to myself, 'How can I be truthful to my character? How can I act a man believed to be fifty-four with an 18-year-old daughter? How do I breathe? What's his rhythm? What does he look like?' I spent ages in my bedsit above an Indian restaurant, pacing, pacing, talking, talking, trying to lose myself, trying to become him. I used to cook myself meals that I thought he would have eaten as a widower. All I was doing was trying to be truthful to my character.'

In that modest room in the northern town, David Suchet put into practise his method of approach to a character that he has used ever since.

But success did not come immediately to the young actor who in the early Seventies found himself face to face with the realities of a precarious profession. When the job offers dried up, he was forced to turn to another source of income to pay his bills. For a time he worked unloading lorries of dogfood, and then became a lift attendant in a block of expensive flats (shades of Poirot's Whitehaven Mansions!).

'It was a manual lift,' he says, 'and for the first week everyone missed their floors! You had to turn the lever the floor below the one you wanted to stop at, and I just couldn't get the hang of it. I remember one poor man who wanted to get out at the sixth floor and I could only get him to either the fifth or the seventh floors. In the end, he got out and walked.'

David was rather more successful when he obtained a position with Moss Bros., the gentlemen's outfitters.

'They gave me a job to sell and hire their formal wear,' he recalls. 'At the time I was very worried that I might never act again, because I had been out of work from November until May, and was starting to feel that the profession was rejecting me. Then suddenly Moss Bros. offered me an apprenticeship as a junior manager. The very morning I had finally decided to accept it, I got a call offering me a part worth £1,000 in the TV series about international detectives, *The Protectors*, with Robert Vaughan and Nyree Dawn Porter, which was shooting in Venice.

'Can you imagine it? One day I was working in Moss Bros. and the next day I was on a plane heading for Venice. I'll never forget when the stewardess offered me champagne on the flight – and I turned it down because I was so broke! Then I realised it was *free*. From London to Zurich I was on my own, as the plane was picking up passengers there, so by the time we reached Venice I was completely legless. I don't even remember going through Customs.

'Mind you, that nine months was a good lesson about keeping your feet on the ground in this profession. While I was at Moss Bros. I actually had a card printed which said 'David Suchet – salesman'. I keep it still, so that I won't be swept away. I'll never allow myself to forget that is where I could go tomorrow.

The success which David has subsequently earned in the theatre, in films and on television make it unlikely that he will ever again need to seek employment in the men's wear business – but the trauma of that period of his life is etched upon his memory.

For almost a decade he worked with the Royal Shakespeare Company, playing many of the classical roles while extending his range in films and TV. His film credits include *The Hunchback of Notre Dame*, *The Falcon and the Snowman*, *Harry and the Hendersons*, *The Last Innocent Man* and *A World Apart*. For television he has done *Oppenheimer*, *Reilly – Ace of Spies*, *The Last Day*, *Being Normal* and the two roles which finally brought him to wider public attention, *The Life of Freud* and *Blott on the Landscape*. Both in their way prepared him for Poirot.

During the making of the BBC 2 series in 1984 about the father of psychoanalysis, David found that he had become so

David Suchet as the father of psychoanalyis.

The character of Freud became 'a sitting tenant I couldn't evict' for David Suchet.

immersed in the role that his conversation was dotted with remarks about psychiatry and comments like 'Freud would have a lot to say about that!' Even today, he admits, the personality of Freud lurks at the back of his consciousness.

'I played him for so long and researched him so much that he was like a sitting tenant I couldn't evict. When I found myself analysing the way my son's nappy was being changed I decided enough was enough. It seems I was not much fun to live with, either, when I was playing him. My family say that I am far nicer at home when I'm playing lighter characters than when I'm playing heavy ones!'

There was certainly nothing so heavy about the eccentric handyman Blott, whom he played two years later in the BBC series *Blott on the Landscape*, based on Tom Sharpe's hilarious farce about urban development and political chicanery. This role marked a major turning part in his fortunes.

'Blott is also still in my head,' he confesses. 'He was a man who showed nothing and yet sometimes revealed everything. But above all else he put me smack bang in the public's eye. If you like, he prepared me for becoming a household name. That's not something I mind – I'm an actor for goodness sake – and I am grateful for it.'

Aside from the public recognition, Blott also earned David the 1986 'Best Actor of the Year Award' from the Royal Television Society and an offer from the producer of the series, Brian Eastman, that he could not refuse – although he did debate with himself for a time. This was the chance to star in Brian's new project for LWT based on the cases of Hercule Poirot.

'I have always been a fan of Agatha Christie's work,' he says, 'and in fact I'd already appeared in a Poirot movie – though not as the detective. In 1985 I played Chief Inspector Japp in *Thirteen at Dinner*, which starred Peter Ustinov.'

David remembers the film mainly for a curiously prophetic incident. He and Ustinov, while in conversation at a cocktail party, were approached by an American television producer who enquired if the famous detective 'had a mini-series in him?' To which Ustinov replied, straight-faced, 'I doubt it – I don't even have my tonsils any more.'

It never crossed David's mind then that he might be offered just such a series, and one playing Poirot, until Brian Eastman put the idea to him after Blott. The idea was initially daunting, because the actor knew he would be following in the footsteps of a number of other high profile figures who had tried to fit into the idiosyncratic little Belgian's tiny black patent spats.

'But then I had to remind myself that I had played Shylock, Iago, Caliban, Bolingbroke and the Fool in Lear, and there had been many brilliant actors who had done those parts, too. The fact hadn't stopped me following *them*. So in fact I was rather used to the feeling and felt I

The eccentric handyman in *Blott on the Landscape*.

could handle it.'

Having seen the films of his two immediate predecessors – Albert Finney and Peter Ustinov – David knew what he was up against.

'Ustinov, with the greatest respect to him, never looked like the Poirot Christie describes because he chose to keep his own colouring while Poirot is dark. On the other hand, Albert Finney's interpretation was wonderful, but it was a very dour and serious performance, and only based on one book.

'I really wanted the part, so to avoid being compared with either Ustinov or Finney I decided to go back to the original novels and short stories. I worked my way through them all – making my lists as I went along, finding out the similarities – and came away with a clear idea of what Agatha Christie wanted from Poirot. Ever since then, whenever I receive a script I get hold of the book or the short story and remind myself of the flavour of it because I've pledged myself to be true to Agatha.

'In the final analysis,' he says, 'it is down to interpretation. One gets sentences like 'Everybody loves to speak to Poirot', and you just read on, forgetting why that should be. As an actor one has to take those sort of sentences on board and think 'Why does everybody like to talk to Poirot?' What is that quality in a person that makes people want to talk to them?'

There was also a single word applied to Poirot that caught David's eye while he was reading the original stories. The word was 'twinkle'.

Poirot's famous twinkle in action.

'If Poirot twinkles, I thought, I can develop that,' he continues. 'As well as everything else, I believe that Poirot does sparkle. He can be fastidious and irritating, but he has the ability to appeal to the lowest as well as the highest in society. I decided to make him charming to even the lowest chambermaid – that would be what would make my portrayal different to the other versions.'

David also had the physical attributes to imitate Poirot. He might not have been cut out to be Cary Grant, but he could fit the role of Poirot in a way no screen heart-throb would be able to come near.

'I knew right from the start I could *look* like him,' David says with a confidence now underlined by eight years of playing the role. 'But it would have been more

David Suchet has to wear a large amount of padding to give him the right shape as Poirot.

difficult for me if I hadn't been a classical actor for so long. There you have to be prepared to look ugly and play ugly if that is what is required.

'Poirot is described in the books as a little man with an egg-shaped head and I can match that without too much make-up. His weight is a slightly different matter, though, because I am quite slim and I have to wear a large amount of padding on my tummy, chest and back and shoulders to give me the right shape. The wing collar helps to make my face look fatter. Believe me, it's quite a relief when all that comes off at the end of a day's filming!'

Before going before the cameras for the first time, however, David also worked on every other aspect of Poirot from the voice to the smallest gesture until he was satisfied he had captured each tiny nuance.

Poirot's accent, in particular, is the result of much thought and experimentation. 'A lot of people have asked me whether the accent is Belgian or French. In fact, in the novels everyone takes Poirot for being French and he always gets very annoyed about this. So obviously his accent can't be pure Belgian because that would sound more like Flemish. It has to be somewhere in-between. So I use a French accent, but very, very slight.'

Visitors to the set of Poirot have frequently been surprised to find David continuing to use this accent even when he is not filming. In fact, he prefers not to switch it on and off between takes.

'I don't find talking in the accent a strain,' he insists. 'Once I'm into the character the accent is easy to maintain. I used to find that if I kept going in and out of the voice it added up to an hour to my working day. But once I go home I switch it off, or otherwise I'd go mad.'

He does, however, remember one incident from the early days of the series with a mixture of amusement and satisfaction.

'I often learn my lines in the car on the way to and from the studio,' he says. 'Once I arrived home and said to my wife, ' 'ello, darling, 'ow are you?' She replied, 'You're speaking with a French accent.' I said, 'No I'm not – its Belgian.' I realised then I was right in character.'

The accent notwithstanding, David still believes the key to his performance is Poirot's moustache.

'The moustache is crucial – it tells you everything about the man,' he says unequivocally, a momentary far-away look coming into his eyes as if remembering the moment a television legend was born. 'It is neat, tidy, groomed and so is Poirot. I had to find the look before I could find the man, and the first time I put the moustache on, I felt myself taking on the personality. Then, and only then, did I really feel I *was* Poirot.

'In the books, of course, the moustache is described variously. In one story it is a stiff, military moustache and in another it is small, tight and very finely curled. If it were as ridiculous as Christie sometimes suggests, then I think people who met him would comment on it, but

Spot the deliberate mistake.

'A thing of beauty.'
Poirot's moustache is
applied for another take.

they don't. To me, the most important thing is what Poirot *himself* says about the moustache. It has to be, in his own terms, a thing of beauty. It must suit the face, because Poirot is a vain man. He has to look, in his own eyes, superb. I really like the moustache. It has become my Poirot.'

David has become equally certain about Poirot's character.

'He is a man of supreme intelligence, a walking brain. He is the greatest lateral-thinking detective ever created in literature – far greater than Sherlock Holmes. That's what fascinated me: once the gruesome part is out of the way we are locked into a great lateral thinker. His way of solving problems is just so off the wall!

'Poirot is also a man settled in his strange world. He loves life, he loves his job and he loves people. He's an endearing, fascinating and infuriating little man. He is also a workaholic. He is insane when he is not working, and that is very like me.

In fact, this is not the only point in common that David has on his list of similarities.

'I'm fairly fastidious, too. We both have an eye for symmetry. I like things in pairs. If I see a picture is awry I can't help putting it straight. And if I put two things on the mantlepiece they have to be exactly evenly space, that sort of thing. I'm tidy, too – I don't like to see muck and dirt anywhere.

'In fact I have become much more tidy as a result of playing Poirot – although I'm not quite so obsessive as he is. Nor am I as fanatical – I certainly don't need the same sized eggs for breakfast as he does! Although I don't think facets of his character have rubbed off on me, that may well be because I am just not aware of it. My wife tells me that it is so, but she still quite likes living with Poirot!'

David's wife, Sheila, is an actress herself, having appeared in a number of popular series including *General Hospital* and *Yes, Minister*. She gave up show business to raise the couple's two children, Robert and Katherine, but in 1990 returned to the West End as understudy to Jane Lapotaire in the box office hit, *Shadowland*. She and David met in the most unforgettable circumstances.

'It was at the Belgrade Theatre in Coventry,' says David with another wry smile. 'We were both in a production of *Dracula*. I was playing Renfield, the little man who sits in his cell – another outsider! I had to eat a fly, a spider and a bird and then go through it all again. It was revolting, not the kind of character you fall in love with. But anyway it was love at first sight for me.'

Despite such an unsavoury start to their relationship, the couple set up home together – but not in a flat or house, but on a 52-foot long, six foot wide sailing barge, the *Prima Donna*, in which they travelled from one theatre engagement to another from 1973 to 1981.

David as James Joyce in the series *Great Writers*.

'I loved the life on the boat,' David recalls fondly. 'I enjoyed travelling on the canals to the places where I was working – Chester, Birmingham and London – and we used to moor the boat close to the theatres. When we started a family we returned to dry land, however – but I've always liked the inland waterways.'

The success of Poirot has now allowed David to buy another boat, which he and the family use to escape from the pressures of fame.

'It is really a get-away-from-it-all type of holiday,' he says, 'and because you are always on the go, if someone recognises me I can be friendly – but I'm not stuck with them forever. This kind of boating makes for marvellous, relaxing days, and the fine scenery along some stretches of waterway would even stun Poirot.'

The long hours that David has had to spend filming each of the series of Poirot has made it difficult to get away onto the

Poirot the gourmet shares a meal with Inspector Japp (Philip Jackson).

boat as often as he would like, but he accepts the demands of his profession with complete equanimity.

'I'm a theatre man, so I'm used to long runs,' he days. 'It's tiring, it's exhausting, but doing a new story and meeting new actors each time keeps the show bubbling and that makes time go very quickly.'

David is also very health conscious, ever since a sharp-eyed viewer noticed that he seemed to have a problem. It is a subject that he discusses frankly and objectively.

'The trouble is your formative years are usually the prelude to the eating habits of a lifetime,' he says. 'Now, I had a real passion for sweet things as a child and there's no doubt that for years my diet as an adult was equally poor. But then in 1987 I got lucky. I was in a television play in the LWT series, *Great Writers*, about James Joyce, and in a 30-second close-up an observant doctor sitting in his armchair at home spotted tell-tale white rings round the irises in my eyes.

'He wrote to me suggesting that I had a check-up. I went to a heart specialist and tests confirmed a dangerously high cholesterol level which could have lead to a fatal stroke. It was the jolt I needed. I was so frightened I became like a monk, gave up all the naughties food-wise, and restricted myself to fresh fruit, salads, a little chicken or grilled fish, the occasional low-fat yoghurt, garlic and lecithin supplements and lemon tea. The result was that my cholesterol level shot down and so did my weight. Since that time I have never been in better shape or more full of energy.

'I owe a great deal to that doctor, who was every bit as observant as Poirot. Perhaps Poirot should take notice of what happened to me because he loves to eat well and likes his food to be rich. I worry about my waistline – but he clearly does *not*!'

Aside from the doctor's warning letter, David has also been on the receiving end of a great deal of fan mail.

'When the series is on, Poirot gets as many as 200 letters a week – the vast majority from ladies,' he says, with the look of a man still slightly surprised at the sheer volume. 'They're not writing to him so much as sex symbol, they're more romantic. A lot of them write to Poirot through me, wishing people had better manners like him. They're not sexy letters, they're more winsome and respectful.'

David has always been totally convinced that Poirot is asexual – a confirmed bachelor and quite happy that way. He says that the little Belgian has an old world charm, but does not believe that he would ever kiss a woman Nonetheless, he still has a tremendous magnetism for females of all ages.

'One of the actresses I worked with a couple of series ago said she loved being with Poirot because she felt one hundred per cent safe,' he recalls. 'If a lady is with him she will be completely protected because there's no ulterior motive behind any of his caring and looking after. He's good company, too, and he'll make sure that if you're in a restaurant, you'll have the finest service. He'll stand up when you go to the cloakroom and he'll stand up when you return.'

David pauses for a moment, as if reflecting on all the things he has learned about the enigmatic figure he has brought to life on the screen, and then continues.

'I believe that an actor has to fall in love with the character. You

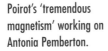

Poirot's 'tremendous magnetism' working on Antonia Pemberton.

have to have a deep, intimate relationship with him, get under the surface. I'm fortunate in that I really do like Poirot. He's a pleasant little man. With the development of the series I've tried to make him lighter, more humorous and witty. And although you must take his brilliance seriously, you can still smile and laugh with Poirot.'

The mention of laughter immediately brings back memories to David of some of the funnier moments that have occurred during the making of the programme. In the first series, for example, Poirot had to step into something unmentionable while investigating the case of a missing person in the Lake District.

'Being a townie, of course, he hates the countryside,' says David, 'and the afront to his dignity when he stood in that huge, smelly cowpat was absolutely hilarious to play.'

Life was not much better for the little detective when he left dry land in the *Problem at Sea*.

'I enjoyed that story enormously, especially because the setting was a boat at sea. But Poirot, of course, is not a very good sailor and he hated it. He is certainly not the best of travellers!'

David smiles, too, at the memory of a scene from a story in the third series, *The Theft of the Royal Ruby*, in which Poirot demonstrated his prowess at mango- peeling at a dinner. Behind this scene lay an actual dinner that David himself had attended as a guest of the Queen and Prince Philip at Buckingham Palace in 1990.

'My table manners were fine until they brought out the fruit,' he smiles. 'I found myself struggling to peel a mango, at which point Prince Philip took over. He cut the mango open with a knife, scooped out the fruit with a spoon and made it all look so easy. I was so impressed by this that I told Brian Eastman and he had one of the scriptwriters include the incident in the story. If you remember, when Poirot was asked by a guest where he had learned his skill at mango peeling, he replied cheekily, 'I was taught by a Duke!'

Thanks to his worldwide success in the series, David and his family now live in a splendid period house on the outskirts of London where, when he has time at home, he likes to pursue his interests in amateur photography, ornithology and playing the clarinet to accompany Sheila on the piano.

'My main love is my family,' he says, his bass voice dropping affectionately, 'and I don't see them half enough because of my commitments. Believe you me, there is nothing more sobering after receiving applause in the theatre or acclaim in the media than to come home and trip over your daughter's sandals in the dark!'

'I value our privacy and I don't like my children being photographed. I don't want them to be seen as 'Poirot's children' and have a hard time at school. In fact, we've had to move twice in recent years – fans were even ringing up the police station for my telephone number and some would knock on the front door at all hours asking for autographs.'

The actor has come a long way from 'David Suchet – salesman' to David Suchet, household name. But no one who meets the man or watches his remarkable transmogrification into the little sleuth on the set can doubt that he has not well earned his fame. He freely admits that his commitment to the series has meant that he has had to turn down a number of big-budget films that might have earned him still greater fame and fortune, but he has no regrets. 'Poirot has given me peace of mind and for first time in twenty years I do not feel insecure.'

David has no doubt the durability of both Agatha Christie and Hercule Poirot.

'Just look at the sales of her books,' he says, 'they are as popular today as they ever were, perhaps more so. No, the public love her murder stories – I don't think we'll ever get tired of them.'

'But having said this, I don't think she ever expected that Poirot would become quite such a star. I know from interviews which I've read about her that she found it difficult to watch her characters being

Drinking to the continued success of Poirot – David with Kika Markham.

portrayed. But my whole approach has been based on the books and for this reason I'd dearly love to have her opinion. I'm sure she would be as surprised as I am that Poirot has become a cult.'

Enjoying the character as David now so obviously does with all the familiarity of having played the role for so long – and warmed by the public reception to it which he has received – David still nurses further ambitions for Poirot.

'One of my aims is to refilm the movies that have already been done,' he says, 'and my mailbag would suggest that the public are really hungry to see me do *Murder on the Orient Express* and *Death on the Nile*. But most of all I would love to leave the full canon of stories on film – that would be a great legacy.'

David Suchet pauses again, and folding his hands neatly together in a gesture very reminiscent of Poirot, makes one last reflection: 'I know a widow who pushes the dining-table to the television and lays two places whenever Poirot is on. On a hard day I remind myself of that and say 'If only one person finds it so important, then pull your socks up and get on with it' As an actor you're in a very powerful position and it must be carefully handled. You affect other peoples' emotions for a moment of their life, so you have a responsibility not to shirk your own.'

THE BIG THREE

BIOGRAPHIES OF POIROT'S COLLEAGUES

CAPTAIN DEPENDABLE

Hugh Fraser who stars as the tall, lean and always immaculately dressed ex-Army officer Captain Arthur Hastings, Poirot's invaluable friend and assistant, has a clear vision of the character he is playing.

'Hastings is very laid back,' Hugh says, with one of the easy smiles that have made him something of a ladies' man both in the series and with female viewers. 'He's really fallen into detective work by chance rather than by any design. Essentially, I suppose, he's a bit of a dilettante.'

For an actor who has played a wide range of roles during his career, ranging from a rocker in the Sixties to villains in the Eighties, Hugh admits to having deliberately avoided watching the earlier screen adaptations of the Poirot cases when he was creating his own interpretation of Captain Hastings, whom he knew had been variously portrayed as a buffoon or simply a stooge of the great detective.

'I hadn't seen either of the Peter Ustinov or Albert Finney versions when I was cast in the series,' he says, 'and I'm glad that I didn't because right from the start I wanted my Hastings to be something quite original.'

Just as it is true to say that David Suchet has reinvented Poirot in the public mind and returned him to the character as envisaged by Agatha Christie, so this is also true of Hugh Fraser's performance, He has made the Captain a dependable and integral part of the little detective's enquiries — and his popularity is evident from the comments he has received from both viewers and critics.

Deborah Thomas of *The Catholic Herald* was one of the earliest reviewers to comment on the importance of his contribution to the series, writing in January 1989, 'The superiority of Poirot extends to the supporting roles. Hugh Fraser as Captain Hastings is an excellent foil.'

Unlike the unequivocal choice of David Suchet to play Poirot, Brian Eastman and the production team took a long while looking for their

Opposite:
Hugh Fraser as
Captain Arthur Hastings.

Captain Hastings. Dozens of actors with the ability to play an ex-Army officer from the First World War who is coming to terms with a changing world outside military life were considered before the part was offered to Hugh. The producer had also given a lot of thought to the way he wanted the character portrayed on the screen.

'It would have been easy to just show him as a bit of a dolt,' Brian recalls, 'but though there are a lot of people who do see Hastings this way, Agatha actually uses him in the books as the voice of the common man. He asks the questions that the reader is asking at any given moment in order to allow Poirot to appear very bright and explain everything.'

Hugh did, however, set himself to read some of the original novels and short stories before filming began, and soon developed his own very particular ideas, which he brought to the series.

'Hastings is a likeable chap,' Hugh continues. 'He's not a great brain, but then he's not a fool either – although he certainly isn't in the same league as Poirot when it comes to the 'little grey cells'.'

Hugh believes that Agatha Christie's love of Sir Arthur Conan Doyle's detective stories has come through in Poirot. 'An obvious parallel for the relationship between Poirot and Hastings would be Holmes and Watson. Poirot, like Holmes, is a lateral thinker, and one of Hastings' functions is to elucidate what is going on in Poirot's mind for the audience. I am certain, too, that it is a working relationship and that Poirot actually employs him.'

The actor's own working life has thrown up as many surprises as he has been confronted with in Poirot. Born in London but brought up in the Midlands, Hugh went straight into drama school at the Webber Douglas Academy before learning his craft in rep in Manchester, Ipswich, Oxford and Edinburgh.

He broke into films and television in the Sixties, playing either hippies or rock singers, he recalls.

'First of all I was a rocker. I had a taste for outlandish clothes and went in for

The Poirot-Hastings relationship has been compared to that of Holmes and Watson.

Hastings the 'likeable chap' and faithful assistant as played by Hugh Fraser.

either crushed velvet or Paisley-patterned bell-bottoms, very tight to the knees and then these enormous flares. I was a wonder of furnishing fabric art! The result was I was always being cast as hippies and the like.'

The immaculate man of today, with his neatly styled hair and faultlessly pressed suit, smiles at the memory of those early years.

'I also had long hair and the sort of expression that went with it. I spent a lot of time as a musician in a group on the road and in London night-clubs. I had got into music when I was at the Traverse Theatre, and actually started by playing the guitar. But I shifted to bass when our bass player was taken ill in the middle of a tour. For a while I actually preferred that to acting, because in 1971 rock 'n' roll was good fun and I loved the music and the life. But I still fitted in the odd acting job as and when it came along.'

Hugh remembers his musical era with wry affection, although he is proud of some of the songs he wrote with the other members of the group. One of their numbers was used as the theme music for the popular children's TV series, *Rainbow*, which started up 1974, However, the crossroads in his career came when he was told that if he wanted a particular part that was available he would have to get his hair cut. His decision was to change his life completely.

'I was offered a role in *Licking Hitler* that required me to have a short back and sides,' he grins. 'I was reluctant to let my flowing locks go, but work was work and so I agreed. Suddenly my career took off. Next I was asked to play Sir Anthony Eden in *Edward & Mrs Simpson*, and although I'd describe myself as lower-middle class by origin I just seemed to graduate effortlessly into aristocratic and upper-middle class types. It's been the same ever since.'

The hippie-turned-gentleman also found himself back in the theatre, appearing in *Teeth 'N' Smiles* as well as a number of classical roles in productions of *Much Ado About Nothing* for the Royal Shakespeare Company, *The Way of the World* at the Chichester Festival and *Hedda Gabler* at the Almeida Theatre.

Then his roles on stage and in films became increasingly those of villains, which gave him a new cause for concern, he says.

'I've played quite a few nasties in my life, and one of the reasons I was so pleased when I was asked to play Captain Hastings was that he was a lighter character – especially after things like *Edge of Darkness*, *Game, Set and Match* and *Jack the Ripper*, which are just three of the things I did before Poirot.'

Hugh has particularly enjoyed being able to play a character who is a bit of a ladies' man – even if many of the women are unattainable or unsuitable – and a great sportsman.

Captain Hastings is never happier than when he is behind the wheel of a car.

'Hastings is obsessed with motor cars and loves to drive his dark green Lagonda. It is something I love, too, because it is such a beautiful motor and the man who owns it manages to keep it in a sort of

lived-in condition, rather than being pristine.'

In between filming episodes of Poirot, Hugh, who lives in London and is married to actress Belinda Lang (who stars in a number of TV series, including *2.4 Children*), has worked on several other TV series, including *Tales of the Unexpected*, *Codename Kyril* and *Smuggler*, with film appearances in *The Draughtsman's Contract*, *Firefox* and *The Missionary*. In July 1991 he had a fascinating opportunity to see television from both sides when he was cast in the chilling BBC drama, *Events at Drimaghleen*, in which a television crew descended on a remote Irish village to try and uncover the truth about a multiple murder case.

'I played the TV producer,' Hugh recalls. 'Naturally I've had plenty of role models in my acting career, and I made him an amalgam of a lot of people. In fact he put his programme before people's feelings and got very tough. He was not choosy about what he did to get his material. The whole group were a bunch of sophisticated TV types, and they caused a lot of trouble in the village. My character was such a contrast to Hastings, who is incapable of doing *anything* nasty.'

He also remembers the film because of the location – a mountainous area outside Belfast. 'On Poirot we are used to elegant surroundings,' he grins. 'On that film we were up to our knees in mud – it poured with rain the whole time we were there!'

Hugh Fraser has every intention of continuing to appear in Poirot for as long as the series continues.

'The role can still develop more,' he says. 'In the early days I did seem to spend a lot of time asking what must have appeared like dumb questions. But as it got a bit repetitive the script writers moved away from that situation. In some of the recent stories Hastings has become much more of an assistant and somebody who in *involved* in the cases.

'Of course he does have a naivety to him. But this is never allowed to become stupidity – rather an endearing quality which Poirot does find a little bit annoying on the one side, though on the other he loves him for it.'

Despite the fact that Captain Hastings only actually appeared in eleven of Agatha Christie's original novels and twenty-six of the short stories, he has undoubtedly become an integral part of the success story of LWT's Poirot.

'The whole experience is one I really enjoy,' adds Hugh, 'and I'm looking forward to ageing gently with David in the later stories. It does make those years as a rocker seem like a lifetime ago, though!'

THE PERFECT MACHINE

The achievement of Pauline Moran, playing Poirot's 'perfect machine' of a secretary, the petite and very formal Miss Lemon, has been to take a character who is little more than a cipher in the original stories and make her a person of flesh and blood who is very much a part of the little detective's life and work.

The role is one that presented a special challenge to Pauline when she accepted the part, and has given her a great sense of satisfaction as a result of its subsequent acceptance by viewers and many Christie purists. Her concept of Felicity Lemon and the elements of their respective characters which have quite a lot in common has also helped to make the part so memorable.

'In a strange way she's a reflection of Poirot,' says Pauline, who with her long red hair and compelling blue eyes is almost unrecognisable from the Miss Lemon of the screen with her little round spectacles and severe, plaited hair-style. 'She has the same fastidiousness and obsession with detail and precision. In fact I am a precise person myself. Not quite to the same degree I must admit, but I have often been likened to a computer because I can remember not only what was said, but the tone of voice in which it was said, twenty years later. I have a great aptitude for minute details, too – so it has been very interesting for me to bring all this to the role.'

In fact Miss Lemon, who Agatha herself said has 'a passion for order almost equalling that of Poirot himself,' is something of a curiosity amongst the authoress's characters because she first appeared as the secretary to a completely *different* detective, Parker Pyne, in two stories written in 1932. She then switched employers to reappear as Poirot's confidential secretary in 'How Does Your Garden Grow?' in *The Regatta Mystery and Other Stories*, published in 1939. In total, she appeared in six short stories and four novels, the first of these being *Hickory Dickory Dock* (1955). It has always been something of a mystery to admirers of Agatha's work why she took so long to give Miss Lemon a role in a full-length novel.

Despite being intended as only a minor figure, Miss Lemon is drawn in typical Christie fashion in a few skilful lines of prose:

Her general effect was that of lots of bones flung together at random... The contents of a letter meant nothing to Miss Lemon except from the point of view of composing an adequate reply... she was very nearly the perfect machine, completely and gloriously uninterested in all human affairs. Her real passion for life was the

Opposite:
Pauline Moran
as Miss Felicity Lemon.

perfection of a filing system beside which all other filing systems would sink into oblivion. She dreamed of such a system at night.

The 'perfect machine', Miss Lemon and her employer.

How Pauline Moran was given the chance to develop this character into an important element of the series makes for a fascinating story – and one again revealed by Brian Eastman.

'As you know, Miss Lemon doesn't appear in all the Poirot stories. In some of them he has a butler, Georges. But at the time I was setting up Poirot I was also involved in the Jeeves series with Stephen Fry and Hugh Laurie. What I didn't want was another series with a butler – so I persuaded the Christie estate that it would be better to develop the character of Miss Lemon and ignore the butler altogether. Thankfully, they agreed, and Pauline has taken what in many other people's hands would have been a very minor and insignificant role and created a fantastic character.

'Although I don't think we've ever spelled it out, the viewer is quite clear about Miss Lemon's status in the series – her aspirations, her liking for Poirot and all the things a great actress brings to a role. The sort of things you could put into the script but would seem rather heavy-handed. But Pauline has managed to bring them all out, although we never wrote a line to that end,' Brian adds.

There is no doubt now that in Pauline Moran the series cast an ideal Miss Lemon, for the Blackpool-born actress shares her character's love of organisation and is also ambitious. Similarly, she is fiercely independent by nature, and self supporting.

'I'm basically a loner,' Pauline explains, 'which stems from my childhood. My mother had me when she was middle-aged and my father died when I was tiny. I had an emotionally repressed upbringing because my mother was so strict. It wasn't that she didn't love me, simply that she was neurotic. The consequence is that I've never truly valued my own self-worth. Anything like that was frowned on at home. I just can't accept a compliment.'

Yet compliments she has certainly received since her training at RADA and her years in rep before breaking into the world of theatre and television. Among her appearances have been leading roles for the RSC in *Troilus and Cressida* and *Mephisto*, plus starring in *Country Life* and *Bedroom Farce* at the Citizens Theatre in Glasgow. Her television roles have included *The Cleopatras*, *The Three Sisters*, *The Prisoner of Zenda* and the thriller about the supernatural, *The Woman in Black*.

Although as Miss Lemon she is almost unrecognisable from her real self, she was recognised in the street after appearing in *The Trespasser*, a TV adaptation of the D.H. Lawrence story with Alan Bates. She was on her way home when a Rolls Royce suddenly pulled up at the kerb.

Pauline Moran in her role as Miss Lemon.

'This voice inside called out to me, 'aren't you that Helena woman from The Trespasser? Gosh you are pre-Raphaelite looking!' And with that the driver sped off!'

In contrast, some of those actually working on Poirot with her have been completely taken aback when seeing her out of costume.

'I remember the occasion of a Christmas party when the film crew didn't recognise me at first. You see I had proper make-up on and I was in nice clothes and my hair was all tarted up!'

As Miss Lemon, Pauline has of course encountered a number of villains during the series, but her memories of the programme are much more-focused on the fashionable clothes which feature in it.

'I love doing the scenes where I get to wear frocks,' she says, her face lighting up again. 'There are also some beautiful ballgowns and evening clothes worn in the series – but not by Miss Lemon because she never gets to leave the office! Although she does dress rather austerely, she is always immaculately turned out. I really *would* like to do more scenes so that I could get to wear more types of clothes!'

Pauline is in fact very interested in fashion, and has a passion for making her own dresses and suits. Indeed, her wardrobe at home is filled with beautiful clothes which she has hand-made.

'I can't remember a time when I wasn't sewing,' she says. 'If I see something way beyond my means which I like then I'll make myself a copy. And what money I save on making dresses, I invest in Victorian jewellery.'

Her expertise with a needle doesn't end there, because she has also made the curtains, lampshades and many of the soft furnishings in her flat.

'I love interior design, too. Stencilling, working with paints and that sort of thing. I also enjoy cooking and entertaining and giving well-presented dinner parties. I suppose that's all part of my fastidiousness.'

Pauline also brings to her role the practical experience of having worked as a secretary when she was not employed as an actress.

'I worked as a secretary with Shell UK in the early Eighties,' she explains, 'and I ended up running the department after about two months. I started off as just a temp and really, because of my skill with computers, I took over.'

Taking over is something she would never consider doing in the employ of Hercule Poirot.

'Miss Lemon is a wonderful secretary and very, very proper with Poirot,' she explains. 'She brings his herb tea at certain times of the day and is precisely punctual. If she was even thirty seconds late both she and Poirot would be horrified!'

The *tisane* which Miss Lemon gives her employer has intrigued many viewers over the years, a number of whom have written in to LWT to enquire precisely what the beverage is she serves. The official explanation is this:

'It is a medicinal tea or infusion made from herbs, originally French, but now readily available here. Mixtures can be taken from your own garden, but health shops sell them in ready-made teabags. Camomile, a sedative and anti-inflamma-

Pauline Moran has a great interest in fashion and finds Miss Lemon's clothes rather austere.

Poirot with a cup of tisane, as prepared by Miss Lemon.

tory agent; fennel for flatulence; mint for indigestion; and lemon balm to soothe are but a few to enjoy.'

Pauline Moran plans to continue serving Poirot with his regular beverage – as well as answering his post and continuing her incredible filing system of his cases, all carefully cross-referenced, of course – as long as the series goes on. Although she is naturally a little worried about public recognition and the loss of privacy that goes with it, she is proud of her achievement in making Miss Lemon something of a cult figure in the series.

Pauline also shares one other fascination with the super-efficient secretary. She is very interested in the occult – everything from the I-Ching to the tarot – and is a skilled astrologer, providing charts for friends on her personal computer.

'I've sometimes wondered if Miss Lemon shares my star sign because of all the similarities between us,' Pauline muses finally. 'I'm a typical Taurean – and I love comfort, beauty and harmony around me. Now where have I heard *that* about somebody

THE HARASSED POLICEMAN

The association between Chief Inspector James Japp of Scotland Yard, played by Philip Jackson, and Hercule Poirot spanned the peak years of the detective's career from 1920 to the late Forties. First introduced in *The Mysterious Affair at Styles* – where Hastings describes him as a 'little, sharp, dark, ferret-face man' – the harassed policeman was last on a case in *The Labours of Hercules* (1947) when Poirot was apparently on the verge of retirement. In total 'Jimmy' Japp, who has a tendency to call the detective 'Moosier Poirot', featured in seven novels and twelve short stories in which he matched wits, invariably without much success, against the little Belgian.

Despite his perpetual worry about being second to the solution of a crime, Japp is a character for whom Philip Jackson has sneaking regard.

'He's a really by-the-book, down-to-earth policeman,' Philip says with the kind of smile that rarely crosses the well-intentioned Chief Inspector's face in the series. 'I do have a certain affection for him because he's quite human, unpretentious and rather child-like.'

Once again in the character of Japp the influence of the Sherlock Holmes stories upon Agatha Christie can be seen at work. For he is very much in the mould of Inspector Lestrade, the Scotland Yard detective with whom Holmes had an uneasy relationship that mixed friendship and frustration, with the policeman mostly coming off second best.

Interestingly, of course, Japp and Poirot had met *before* fate brought them together again in Styles St Mary. Their paths had crossed in 1904, when Poirot was still working for the Belgian police, as Japp reminisces in *The Mysterious Affair at Styles*:

He and I worked together – the Abercrombie forgery case – he was run down in Brussels. Ah, those were great days, moosier. Then, do you remember 'Baron Altara'? There was a pretty rogue for you! He eluded the clutches of half the police in Europe. But we nailed him in Antwerp – thanks to Mr Poirot.

Casting Chief Inspector Japp was also not finalised until a lot of actors had been seen and considered for the role. Here again with a stereotyped public image of the policeman as a kind of Mr Plod character, the

Opposite:
Inspector Japp 'the down-to-earth policeman' as played by Philip Jackson.

The relationship between Japp and Poirot is another important element in the success story of the series.

Philip Jackson has broken the mould of Japp as the plodding policeman.

production team were anxious to break the mould.

Brian Eastman explains: 'It would be very easy to play Japp as a plodding copper, but that is not how we saw the character or how we wanted to write him. In fact, Japp has a very sparky sort of relationship with Poirot all the time – there is a lot of rivalry there, but also an enormous amount of affection.'

Philip Jackson was finally picked for the part because of his ability to balance the policeman's by-the-book style with an extra intelligence and individual character. The energetic and versatile actor brought a lifetime of experience in the theatre, in films and on television to giving Japp his unique appeal.

Born in Nottingham, Philip did not get hooked on acting until he was at Bristol University studying a rather unusual combination of subjects – drama and German.

'I really didn't want to act until that point. In fact,' he says with a broad grin, 'I just did drama because it seemed like a better alternative to the idea of getting a 'proper' job! But I did a lot of plays there and enjoyed them. So when I left Bristol I wrote to a few companies for work and was offered a job by Liverpool Playhouse.

'It was there that I got my experience of playing in rep, and I stayed with the company for eighteen months. Gradually I got better and better parts, until finally the time seemed right for me to move to London. Since then I've had a lot of interesting roles, though Japp has been the longest and probably got me more publicity than any of the others.'

Amongst Philip's theatrical appearances have been *Rat In The Skull* at the Royal Court, *A Midsummer Night's Dream* with the Royal Shakespeare Company and the starring role of Frank in *Forget Me Not Lane* at the Greenwich Theatre. On films he has been seen in *The Fourth Protocol* and *High Hopes*, while his earlier TV work included *Blooming Youth*, *Robin of Sherwood* and *The Dark Room*.

Philip particularly relished the opportunity to play Japp, because he had been an avid reader of Agatha Christie from the age of nine.

'I really enjoyed the way she wrote such clever plots,' he says. 'The fact that she doesn't go into great depth with her characters means that they can easily become simplified in people's minds. The challenge to an actor is to give the character a depth above and beyond what is on the printed page.'

More than one television critic has give Philip credit for doing just that – Deborah Thomas of *The Catholic Herald*, writing in January 1990: 'Philip Jackson as Inspector Japp is sufficiently unattractive

The 'sparky' effect of Poirot on Japp.

Poirot and Japp combine forces on another case.

without being too stupid to be a fit rival for the great Belgian.'

Philip admits, however, that his achievement is not down to the same kind of methodical research as his co-star.

'Unlike David, I didn't research the part at all,' he says. 'I knew the books, of course, but I preferred to take the character from the scripts alone. Actually I'm not much like Japp – I haven't really got a moustache for a start!'

Philip has, however, come to understand Japp very well.

'He's dedicated to his job and absolutely honest and straightforward. He's sort of friends with Poirot in a strange kind of way, although he is certainly irritated by the fact that the Belgian detective keeps beating him. In some ways their friendship is surprising when you think of how different their methods of solving crime are – Poirot is methodical and orderly while Japp tends to be a bit haphazard.'

The actor has also developed a close working relationship with David Suchet, which has given their scenes together such a *frisson*.

'David is Poirot when he's filming and this makes everyone raise their own performances. The scriptwriters and production people have also taken a lot of trouble to get the authentic feel of the Thirties in the costumes and the settings.

'I love the 1936 period, especially the architecture. I've spent some time in New York, both working and staying with friends, and there is a lot of Art Deco stuff there which I adore. so finding myself among the same things when I'm filming is an added bonus.'

Apart from the satisfaction gained from his role in Poirot, Philip also became a father again while making the second series. In September

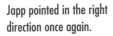

Japp pointed in the right direction once again.

The inspector tackles another suspect, (Jonathan Firth) in *Hickory Dickory Dock*.

1990, he and his actress wife Sally Baxter had a daughter, Amy, which they had not thought would be possible after the Caesarean birth of their son George, then aged five. When he is not working or looking after the children, Philip is a keen squash and snooker player and enjoys reading and watching films.

'The people associated with Poirot are a great team and I'm happy to go on with the series,' he says. 'Japp isn't involved in all of Poirot's cases, of course, so I've no idea how many more episodes I might be asked to do. But there are still quite a few of the novels left to adapt, and I've no doubt that the series has a good few more years to run.'

One of Chief Inspector Japp's lines from the original books remains imprinted on Philip memory. He feels it somehow summarises the mixture of rivalry and admiration that is the key to the Poirot/Japp relationship: 'I shouldn't wonder' the policeman declares to his friend, 'if you ended by detecting your own death... That's an idea, that is. Ought to be put in a book.'

THE MANY FACES OF HERCULE POIROT

If fate had decided otherwise, Hercule Poirot would have made his first appearance outside the printed page in a play in which he was twenty years younger, was very attractive to young girls who were forever falling in love with him, and been renamed Beau Poirot. This transformation of his persona was, in fact, the intention of playwright Michael Morton when he was commissioned by the London theatrical producer Gerald du Maurier to adapt Agatha Christie's novel *The Murder of Roger Ackroyd* for the stage in 1928.

Morton, who already had a considerable reputation as a skilful adapter of novels, believed that the 1926 village murder mystery which had established its authoress's fame would not work on the stage in its present form. The story, set in King's Abbot, which begins with the apparent suicide of a wealthy widow named Ferrars and lures Poirot – now living in the village cultivating his garden instead of solving crimes – back into doing what he does best, seemed to lack the necessary drama for a theatre audience. This despite its brilliantly deceptive ending, which fellow crime writer Dorothy L. Sayers had declared was 'fair – but fooled you!'

Despite her undeniable pleasure at the idea of one of her books appearing on the stage, Agatha Christie 'much disliked' Morton's suggestion and insisted that Poirot had to retain the characteristics which she believed had make him unique among contemporary fictional detectives. Although she won her argument, Agatha still had to allow the removal of one of the other pivotal characters, Caroline Sheppard, the spinster sister of the local doctor, who instead became a pretty, romantic young thing – though at least she was not asked to fall in love with Poirot! Much of the action was also switched to focus around the discovery of the body of Roger Ackroyd, stabbed to death in his study

THE GRAPHIC, June 9, 1928

EXPRESSIONS OF A SLEUTH

Close-ups of Mr. Charles Laughton as Hercule Poirot in "Alibi" at the Prince of Wales Theatre

Mr. Charles Laughton, the twenty-six-year-old actor as he is in real life

"Monsieur l'Inspecteur, il est bête comme ——" Poirot is amused at the clumsy methods of the local police

"Englishmen conceal only one thing—their love." The detective in one of his philosophical moods as a rest from sleuthing

"I appeal to you, Mees Flora—tell me ze truth." The relentless Poirot in plaintive mood

"Each one of you has something to hide." Poirot grows suspicious of everybody

Poirot at work. The effective curtain to Act I, when the detective sits alone in front of the murdered man, turns down the lights, and mentally reconstructs the crime

"Poirot may play the fool, but there is a reason behind his actions," he says to the unsuspecting criminal

"To me it grows clearer." Poirot has a clue which he keeps to himself

"Ze person who killed Sir Ackroyd is in zis room." The detective in one of his "je sais tout" moods

after dinner.

The play, retitled *Alibi*, opened on 15 May, 1928 at the Prince of Wales' Theatre with Charles Laughton, an actor of rapidly growing reputation, appearing as the first of what has become a continuing line of performers interpreting Poirot. It also marked the debut of Agatha Christie's work on the London stage, which she has continued to dominate to the present day – most famously with *The Mousetrap*, 'the world's longest running play', now in its forty-third year at St Martin's Theatre.

Laughton played Poirot as a youthful, somewhat portly figure, with slicked-down hair and a tiny moustache, and switched effortlessly from a suit with a carnation button-hole to a dinner jacket and bow tie during the unfolding of the mystery. He approached the part in his usual manner, little realising that he was attempting to create a man destined to become an archetype.

'I interpreted Poirot the best way I knew how,' he reflected years later, 'which is the way I play every part. My idea of things may be wrong in the minds of some purists, but on stage I can only give forth my own ideas.'

Laughton's 'own ideas' of the character earned the play mixed notices. *The Times* reviewer, for example, asking whether it was possible to make a play out of 'a theoretical analysis' and then answering himself: 'If we do not weary of Poirot shooting questions to the right and left, Poirot with uplifted finger expounding his views to a half-circle of listeners, it is because Mr Charles Laughton, with little help from the text, makes a personality out of the fat and sentimental little *ratiocinator*.

The authoress, who attended the first night, was not so impressed by the personality of her detective on the stage. 'Mr Laughton is a good actor,' she said bluntly, 'but entirely unlike Hercule Poirot.'

Despite the critics' and Agatha Christie's reservations, the public loved *Alibi* and it ran for 250 performances at the Prince of Wales, before being transferred across the Atlantic in February 1932 under the auspices of the 'boy wonder' producer of the Broadway stage, Jed Harris.

Although Agatha Christie was not exactly ecstatic about the debut of Poirot in the theatre, she had been bitten by the theatrical bug. And while *Alibi* was still bringing in the crowds she set about devising a second stage appearance for her detective – though this time she was going to write the play herself. The original work was entitled *Black Coffee*, and she later described it in her autobiography as a conventional spy thriller. 'Although full of cliches, it was not, I think, at all bad,' she wrote.

The drama about the murder of a scientist and the theft of a secret formula for making deadly weapons which Poirot neatly solves by pure logic opened in December 1930 at the Embassy Theatre, London and starred Francis L. Sullivan as an even more heavyweight Poirot than his predecessor. A man over six-feet tall who weighed nineteen stone, with heavy, florid features and a booming voice, Sullivan had made a speciality of playing master criminals and oily villains before switching sides to the law as the Belgian detective.

Whether audiences were any more or less happy with Sullivan's portrayal of the dapper detective, they were keen enough to keep *Black Coffee* running for over 100 performances. The *Daily Telegraph* reviewer, for one preferred his performance to that of Charles Laughton, while the man from *The Times* applauded the actor's 'contribution to the evening's entertainment – which is a considerable one.'

The authoress herself, however, was abroad that Christmas and could not visit the Embassy until the New Year. Again she was not very happy with what she saw, puzzling: 'It always seems strange to me that whoever plays Poirot is an outsized man.'

When Agatha later met Francis Sullivan and his wife, however, she was instantly charmed by the big, gregarious man and the two became firm friends. Soon she was a frequent visitor to the Sullivans' home at Haslemere in Surrey, where she delighted in listening to the actor's many colourful stories about his life and career.

If Laughton and Sullivan were somewhat unlike the fictional Poirot on account of their girth, the actor who brought him to the screen was completely dissimilar because of his height, appearance *and* looks. Austin Trevor, the cinema's first Poirot, was tall, dark and handsome – not to mention clean-shaven – and appeared on screen as a typical Thirties type hero, who outsmarted criminals because he was smarter and charmed the ladies because he was charming.

Austin, who made his debut in the screen version of *Alibi*, filmed by Real Art Studios in 1931, had built his reputation as a character actor working at Stratford-on- Avon with the Shakespeare Festival Company and at the Old Vic as well in a series of plays by John Galsworthy. And

Footnote: *Black Coffee* has remained a popular play with repertory and amateur dramatic societies ever since the early stage and film versions. It was, for example, very successfully toured in 1951 with the stylish actor Kenneth Kent creating a fastidious Poirot complete with twirled moustache and arched eyebrows; and thirty years later another company with the urbane and witty Patrick Cargill from Thames Television's long-running series, *Father, Dear Father* as the detective played to packed theatres all over the country throughout 1981.

yet despite the variety of his subsequent work in radio, on films and in television, he is probably still best remembered for having starred as the most unlikely Poirot in three films: *Alibi* (1931) and *Black Coffee* (1931), both adapted from the stage plays, and *Lord Edgware Dies* (1934) from the 1933 novel of the same title.

'I had only just got into movies and was happy to play the character any way I was asked,' Austin was to admit to an interviewer some years later. 'I was never quite sure why they cast me as Poirot – it may have had something to do with the fact I had played the French detective, Inspector Hanaud, in *At The Villa Rose*, filmed the previous year. I think that the producer had decided that a fat, foreign detective would not appeal to British cinema audiences, so they made Poirot a typical clean-cut Thirties hero.'

To be fair to Austin, he had already gained a reputation in show business for his fluency in several languages as well as his ability to portray various ethnic types in English. All of which was a long way from his birth as Trevor Schilsky in 1897 in one of the poorer districts of Belfast and his stage debut at eighteen playing the ghost in a production of *Hamlet*!

Alibi, Austin's first appearance as Poirot, was adapted from Michael Morton's stage play by Leslie Hiscott, who also directed the picture. In a curious twist of fate it was filmed at Twickenham Studios where almost sixty years later David Suchet would create the definitive Poirot! The producer was Julius Hagan, who had secured the rights after attending one of Charles Laughton's performances in London. There is no evidence that Hagan even considered offering Laughton the chance to repeat his role on the screen; indeed there is every indication that he wanted to portray a very different kind of detective on the screen – and one that was equally unlike Agatha Christie's original.

The film, which co-starred Elizabeth Allen, Clare Greet and the lugubrious Franklyn Dyall, was nonetheless popular at the box office, with the review in *The Times* perhaps best explaining the reason for this: 'The film nowhere departs from the beaten track of detective stories and is, in its own kind, a reasonable and competent piece of work.'

Julius Hagen wasted no time after this encouraging reception and before the summer was out he had Agatha's original play, *Black Coffee*, before the cameras in Twickenham, once again adapted by director Leslie Hiscott. The picture also introduced the first Hastings and Japp of the screen, in the form of character actors Richard Cooper and C.V. France.

Austin Trevor was evidently more at home with the role of Poirot in this second outing, and apart from charming the lovely Adrienne Allen

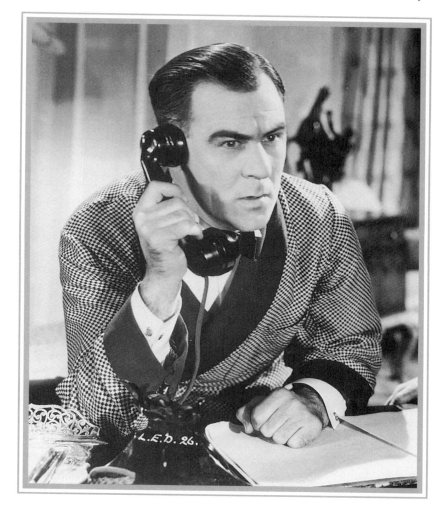

Austin Trevor, the first
screen Poirot in *Lord
Edgware Dies.*

and preventing her from drinking the fatal cup of black coffee,
unmasked the real villain in a dramatic scene in which he appeared to
drink the poison himself. Although the *Daily Mail's* reviewer found
some of the elements in the mystery difficult to swallow, he conceded
that the star had made Poirot a 'watchable and ingenious detective.'

Two years passed before Austin Trevor played the role for the third
and last time. With no new stage adaptation to fall back on, Julius
Hagan bought the rights to what was then Agatha's latest novel, *Lord
Edgware Dies.* As a matter of interest, the authoress had been inspired
to write this story after watching a performance in London of the
American monologist Ruth Draper, who impressed her very much by
her ability to 'transform herself from a nagging wife to a peasant girl
kneeling in a cathedral.'

In *Lord Edgware Dies* (retitled *Thirteen At Dinner* in America) Poirot was confronted with the murder of the estranged nobleman of the title and a wide variety of suspects including Lady Edgware, several actors and a trained impersonator, Carlotta Adams. A chance remark by a stranger in the street finally put him onto the track of the killer. Richard Cooper again co-starred as the faithful Captain Hastings, with Jane Carr as Lady Edgware.

The style of this third Poirot film was certainly different to its predecessors, mainly due to the fact that a new director, Henry Edwards had taken over from Leslie Hiscott. Edwards, more adept at romantic stories than murder mysteries, failed to inject any real tension into the picture and severely laboured the final denouement. Neither the critics or audiences warmed to *Lord Edgware Dies*, and there the series ended.

Austin Trevor, for his part, went on to enjoy a number of starring roles in several Broadway plays as well as two very successful movies, *Goodbye Mr Chips* (1939) and *The Red Shoes* (1948). But he was not quite finished with the role he first brought to the screen. In 1956 he made his last film appearance, in the MGM version of *The Alphabet Murders*, in which the American actor Tony Randall filled the shoes he had once worn.

'It is quite a twist of fate to find myself back in a film about Hercule Poirot' Austin said during the filming of the picture at Pinewood. 'Mine is only a small part so I have plenty of time to watch Tony Randall playing him. He's certainly a lot more like the character in the books than I was – but then tastes have changed a great deal since then!'

The next attempt by film makers to initiate a series of Poirot films began in 1966, but sadly was also to fall short of its high ideals through a mixture of mis-casting and poor scriptwriting. MGM were the studios behind the project and they selected the 1935 novel, *The ABC Murders*, to be the first of what it was hoped would be a series of pictures all filmed in England to match the popularity of their earlier quartet of movies in the early sixties featuring Miss Marple. In these, the redoubtable Margaret Rutherford had made Agatha's other famous sleuth a box office triumph – despite the fact that she bore little resemblance to the original character of the books – and even though the film-makers had actually appropriated the plots of a pair of Poirot novels as the basis of two of the films, *Murder at the Gallop* and *Murder Most Foul*.

Initially, though, the omens for the picture looked good. *The ABC Murders* with its catalogue of seemingly motiveless crimes which are only linked by the victims' initials, had been described as 'a masterwork of carefully concealed artifice' and showed Poirot at the very top of his deductive form. The plot also provided a much more substantial and involved role for Captain Hastings.

According to film historian Philip Jenkinson, the picture – entitled *The Alphabet Murders* to avoid confusion with the English ABC cinema chain – was originally to have been directed by Seth Holt, with the American comedian, Zero Mostel, from a *A Funny Thing Happened on the Way to the Forum* (1963) in the leading role. Once again, it seemed, another bulky and larger-than-life Poirot was to be foisted on the public. 'Mostel was retained and an adaptation made,' Jenkins explains, 'which included a bedroom scene for Poirot. Agatha Christie

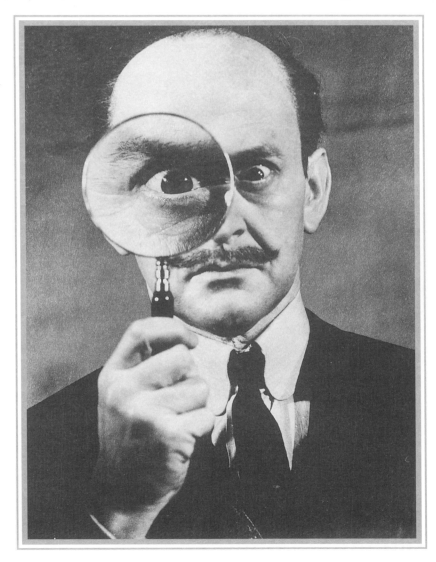

Tony Randall as Poirot in
The Alphabet Murders.

was not amused, and the production was abandoned on what was to have been the first day of shooting.'

The authoress was certainly *not* amused and told MGM so in no uncertain terms. 'I will not have Poirot turned into some sort of gorilla or private eye,' she said. 'Anyway, if people have liked Poirot for about forty years as an egocentric creep they would probably prefer him to go on that way.'

Once relations between the two parties had been healed as a result of reassurances from MGM that they would not take such liberties with Poirot, the project went ahead. A new director, the American Frank Tashlin, was chosen, and for Poirot he cast Tony Randall, previously best known for his comedy roles. Born in Oklahoma in 1920, Tony had built himself a reputation as an urbane, intelligent character actor, familiar to the public for his television role Felix Unger in *The Odd Couple* and in films such as *Will Success Spoil Rock Hunter?* (1957), *Pillow Talk* (1959) and the much under-rated *Seven Faces of Dr Lao* (1964).

Tony had, in fact, worked with Frank Tashlin before and readily accepted the role of Poirot – though he realised right from the start it was a part fraught with difficulties.

'I knew Poirot had been played before, but not very well,' he was to recall later in an interview with Michael Buckley of *Films in Review*. 'It seemed to me I should find out how Agatha Christie had described him. In one of the early books there is a portrait of him – exactly like her description: he's bald, has a big nose, moustache and a pot belly. The clothes, too, he's very careful about those, so it was important to make him look debonair. I felt comfortable in the picture, it was fun. It may not have been terribly good, but I enjoyed it.'

On the set at Elstree Studios, Tony Randall struck up an immediate raport with his co-star, the plump, veteran English comedy actor Robert Morley, playing Hastings, who was already familiar with the oeuvre having worked with Margaret Rutherford in *Murder at the Gallop*. And in an attempt to try and please all the purist fans of Hercule Poirot, Tony took a lot of trouble with his make-up, changing the shape of his nose and raising his hairline almost to the point of baldness.

Although it is true to say that the script by David Pursall and Jack Seddon – who had worked on the earlier Miss Marple films – did preserve some of the ingenuity of the original novel, it was the intro-duction of comic elements that too often spoiled the mood of the story. Always the realist, Tony Randall suspected that *The Alphabet Murders* would please neither Agatha Christie or the press – and he was right. *The New York Times* encapsulated the general feeling of disappoint-ment:

Neither Mr Randall's Poirot, nor the gags, chases, and red herrings offered, are inventive, comical or charming enough to make this more than a routine run-through of cliches and clues. What the director and his writers and cast have failed to do is to make Poirot and his intriguing gallery of friends and foes the classic characters that have genuinely fascinated millions of Agatha Christie readers all these years. Poirot in pictures is simply an unexciting, bizarre 'Belgian with a beak' involved in murders that are not especially exciting

Almost ten years were to pass before those words were to be disproved as a result of another equally surprising piece of casting and a performance that would set a benchmark for subsequent portrayals...

Murder on the Orient Express (1934) has long been regarded as one of Agatha's best known and most popular books. Based on the famous railway journey from Paris to Istanbul which the authoress herself first made in 1928, the plot involved Poirot in a *tour de force* of detection, unravelling the murder of a wealthy American traveller on the train. Two real events had actually inspired Agatha to write the book: reports of a terrible blizzard which had left the Orient Express snowbound near the Turkish border in 1929 and the brutal kidnapping of Charles Lindburgh's son in 1932. *The Times Literary Supplement* led the critics' cheers when the novel first appeared: 'The little grey cells solve once more the seemingly insoluble.'

There is evidence that for nearly forty years Agatha Christie had resisted all approaches by film makers both English and American for permission to film *Murder on the Orient Express*. Indeed, it took the persuasive powers of a friend, Lord Mountbatten, to get the authoress finally to agree to let his son-in-law, the producer John Brabourne, make the picture in 1974. The result was a spectacularly successful movie, faithful to the original, and with such a unique performance by Albert Finney in the starring role that he won not only the Best Actor award from BAFTA but was also nominat-

Albert Finney with Sir John Gielgud in *Murder on the Orient Express*.

Albert Finney won the Best
Actor award from BAFTA
for his role as Poirot.

ed for an Oscar. It was undoubtedly the most accurate interpretation of
any of Agatha's works to that date, and can also be seen to have
marked a turning point in Christie-on-the-screen.

Directed with great panache by Sidney Lumet from Paul Dehn's
screenplay – and filmed largely on location in wintery Yugoslavia using
carriages that had been borrowed from *Compagnie Internationale de
Wagons-lits Museum* in France – *Murder on the Orient Express* was

notable for its great attention to detail. None more so than in Albert Finney's performance as Poirot – a piece of casting that initially surprised purists as much as it did the young actor himself. (He was thirty-eight at the time.) Finney has subsequently admitted that it was his admiration for Lumet that made him take on the role and thereby land himself with an exhausting daily make-up routine in the hands of specialist Charles Parker.

'It took me two hours in make-up every morning before I could play Poirot,' he recalled some time later. 'Facially, the transformation was achieved with a false nose – my own is too tilted for Poirot – and padded cheeks to achieve the egg-shaped look. But by far the most important part of the make-up was the gleaming black hair and meticulously trimmed and waxed period moustache. Poirot's moustache is always ferociously waxed into points at the end, and he uses a certain 'tonic' – not a 'dye' – to keep his hair perennially young-looking. I had to apply lashings of hair cream mixed with black powder, and although the effect was amazing it took four shampoos to get it off every night!

'In order to create Poirot's short, solid look I wore body padding – a T-shirt draped with cotton wool. I even had to have padded thighs to make me look wide so that my own height appeared less – and by the time I got on the set I looked twenty years older and thirty pounds heavier! It was really tough shooting in the cramped interior of the train under all the lamps – and I would get so hot by lunchtime that I'd leave my padding in the fridge during the break to cool off!'

Finney's search for authenticity even went as far as the manner in which he spoke as the detective. 'Poirot's English is deliberately imperfect because he has learned that the English can be tricked into saying things heedlessly through their disparaging attitude towards foreigners. So the general reaction to his interrogations was that anyone who looked and spoke as he did in the Twenties and Thirties could be easily outwitted. Then, suddenly, when he has solved his case and is speaking in front of the suspects, Poirot's English improves. It is as if his accent has been sharpened along with his wits during the stimulating mental exercise of solving a crime through the logical process of deduction.'

The picture's success was due not only to Albert Finney's absorbing performance, but also to the ensemble acting of the international galaxy of co-stars playing the suspects, including John Gielgud, Sean Connery, Lauren Bacall, Ingrid Bergman, Anthony Perkins, Vanessa Redgrave, Wendy Hillier, Martin Balsam and Richard Widmark. *The Times* reviewer echoed the comments of most critics when he declared, '*Murder on the Orient Express* is touchingly loyal to Mrs Christie and to the period – it also demands the same adjustments, the same precarious suspension of disbelief.'

Agatha Christie, who attended the gala premiere in London and the banquet afterwards – her last public event before her death – had only one reservation.

'The film was well made except for one mistake,' she told journalists with a twinkle in her eye. 'It was Albert Finney as my detective Hercule Poirot. I wrote that he had the finest moustache in England – and he didn't in the film. I thought that a pity – *why* didn't he?'

For the star himself, one encounter with Poirot was enough. Albert Finney made it quite clear that despite the success of the picture he would not play the detective again and, in any event, he was anxious to return to working in the theatre. This said, his role as the little detective remains a landmark and one of which he is proud.

'There were a lot of good reasons for me *not* to have done the film,' he reflects today. 'But right from the start Sidney Lumet was clear about what he wanted and it was a marvellous way to work. Everybody stayed sharp and quick-witted during the shooting, which is just what a good film needs – especially a murder mystery.'

Albert Finney's award-winning performance as Hercule Poirot made him a difficult act to follow. Having failed to get Finney to change his mind, producer John Brabourne searched long and hard to find another actor with the skill to bring the Belgian detective to life again on the screen under the shadow cast by his predecessor. After considering an extensive list of names, he finally settled on the versatile and gifted 56 year-old Peter Ustinov. When accepting the role, Peter knew that although he was physically unlike the Poirot of fiction, he still felt he had the ingenuity and degree of eccentricity necessary to create a new interpretation of the sleuth.

The result of this decision has meant that Ustinov is now second only to David Suchet in the number of times he has played Poirot on the screen. His total is six: three adaptations for the cinema and the same number for television. The experience has given him a special insight into the detective's character, not to mention some idiosyncratic views about him.

'He is a very engaging character, although he's quite awful really,' Peter says, with the sort of twinkle in his eye that makes any interviewer unsure as to just how seriously he wants to be taken. 'I should hate to know him. He's very vain, self- contained and finicky. He's also very avaricious, very honourable and very deeply in love with himself. And he's so terribly accurate and tidy in his mind and habits.

'Poirot is the sort of man who has a little sewing kit with him at all

Poirot is a very engaging character, but quite awful according to Peter Ustinov in *Death on The Nile*.

times so that an offending button on his underwear – that can be seen by nobody. – can be replaced at a moment's notice. That's quite a strain for an actor to play – especially someone who's not ordered like that such as me!'

Peter recalls clearly developing Poirot's accent which, as an expert mimic, he deliberately made more extravagant than any of his predecessors.

'On the printed page, Poirot is no more Belgian than Major Thompson is English,' he reflects. 'In language terms we probably see him as one of those foreign schoolmasters whose English is too correct – all very fluent and fluid and quite artificial. Remember that Poirot only puts the simplest words into French, the complex ones are always left in English.

'I actually used a genuine Belgian accent for the role – it came from listening to the Belgian Ambassador to Paris. He does not drop his 'hs' Instead he adds them where they are not supposed to be, which is how a Belgian might talk.'

The attention to detail which had been a feature of *Murder on the Orient Express* was similarly employed by John Brabourne in Peter's debut as Poirot in *Death on the Nile*, based on the exotic 1937 novel. Location filming was undertaken in Egypt at a number of places, including Cairo, Aswan, Karnak and Luxor, while a 138-foot Egyptian cruiser was hired and adapted as the setting for the series of murders which – like the mystery on the train – had been inspired by trips Agatha had made along the Nile both as a child and with her husband, Max.

Once more an impressive list of international stars were hired to play the suspect – including David Niven, Bette Davis, Maggie Smith, Mia Farrow, Jack Warden and Angela Lansbury. The screenplay was faithfully rendered from the novel by Anthony Shaffer and the picture atmospherically directed by John Guillerman. *Death on the Nile* was again warmly welcomed by the press – 'terrific escapist entertainment', was the *Daily Express* verdict – while Peter Ustinov's performance was commended for not trying to imitate that of Albert Finney, although still offering audiences 'the inimitable and indomitable sleuth dear to Agatha Christie fans'. Shortly after the picture opened, Peter was voted Best Actor of the Year for his role by the Variety Club of Great Britain.

Unlike his predecessor, Peter was happy to go on playing the role, and in 1981 filmed *Evil Under The Sun*, in which he made the detective a wittier if rather more flamboyant character. Changes were also made to Agatha's original 1941 mystery novel about the discovery of a woman's body strangled on the Devon coast. Scriptwriter Anthony Shaffer shifted the setting to the fashionable Adriatic coast – although the filming actually took place mainly on Majorca. The director was Guy Hamilton, a master of the glossy locale, who was familiar to many cinema-goers for his work on four of the James Bond films. Amongst the cast of 'suspects' this time were James Mason, Diana Rigg, Jane Birkin,

A galaxy of co-stars appeared with Peter Ustinov in *Death on the Nile.*

Ustinov in *Evil Under The Sun*.

Roddy McDowall, Sylvia Miles and Colin Blakely, plus a return appearance of Maggie Smith.

Although *Evil Under The Sun* did not prove quite as successful at the box office as its predecessor, Ustinov had undoubtedly created a distinctive Poirot, and took considerable pleasure from being told at the premiere by the Queen that Poirot was 'one of her favourite fictional detectives' and she had really enjoyed his interpretation on the screen.

The third of the big-budget Poirot movies, *Appointment With Death*, was also set in an exotic location and again adapted by Anthony Shaffer from a novel (originally published in 1938) set around Petra, the former centre of the Arab Kingdom, which Agatha and her husband had visited during one of their Middle East journeys in the early Thirties. The book was also highly regarded by enthusiasts for the appearance of Mrs Boynton, who has been described as the most convincing and evil character in any of the authoress's novels.

The story about a murder plot which Poirot overhears one night during a holiday in the Holy Land provided several more intriguing roles for leading stars, including Lauren Bacall, Carrie Fisher, Hayley Mills, Michael Sarrazin and Sir John Gielgud. Michael Winner directed the picture, shot primarily in Israel, with Peter seeming even more at home in his role.

'Playing Poirot has become a little like playing Bach on the violin,' he told one journalist on location. 'You have to say the same thing all the time, but do it differently. You have to relax into the part.'

Appointment With Death did not mark the end of Ustinov's association with Poirot. In 1985, Warner Brothers, the American TV and film-

Ustinov as Poirot in
Appointment with Death.

making conglomerate, launched the first of three made-for-television cases in which Ustinov also starred. The first of these was entitled *Agatha Christie's 13 At Dinner*, a ninety-minute adaptation by Rod Browning of the old Austin Trevor favourite, *Lord Edgware Dies*. Produced by Neil Hartley and directed by Lou Antonio, the story had, however, been somewhat updated, with Poirot now meeting the female impersonator at the heart of the mystery while both of them were guests on the David Frost TV Show! Co-starring with Peter were Faye Dunaway, John Stride, Lee Horsley and a certain David Suchet, playing 'the not terribly bright Inspector Japp of Scotland Yard', according to one review of the transmission. *The New York Times*' verdict of Ustinov's switch to the small screen was guarded, though it conceded that he 'kept the action percolating nicely, a special wardrobe draping his consider-able girth'.

This television adaptation also introduced a new Captain Hastings, played by the American actor, Jonathan Cecil, who was singled out for praise by the US critic John J. O'Connor. 'Making Mr Ustinov look especially good is Jonathan Cecil, who plays Hastings, M Poirot's faithful and zanily humble friend.' he wrote. 'A model of English reserve, Hastings is always fussing over the nonplussed Poirot. Watch the little bit as the great detective, preparing to make his entrance on the Frost show, fends off the overprotective Hastings. It is the kind of nutty detail that make *13 At Dinner* a pleasant diversion.'

A year later, Warner Brothers screened an even longer adaptation, *Dead Man's Folly*, based on the 1956 novel in which Poirot is teamed with Ariadne Oliver to solve a murder mystery game which has become real – all played out against the background of Nasse House, which Agatha based on her own Devonshire home, Greenway House. Filmed entirely in the UK, the two hour film scripted by Rod Browning and directed by the English director, Clive Donner, co-starred Jean Stapleton as Mrs Oliver, Tim Piggott-Smith as the owner of the country house, plus Susan Wooldridge, Nicolette Sheridan and Constance

Cummings. Jonathan Cecil returned as Hastings, although in a some-what smaller role than he had in the previous film.

Despite *Dead Man's Folly* being shown in Britain on Christmas Day, 1986, it received the same mixed reviews it had done in America, where *The New York Times* had decided: 'Perhaps *Dead Man's Folly* is a trifle too complicated to fit comfortably into a format that, with time out for commercials runs less than one hour and forty minutes... And for the most part, Mr Ustinov looks even more irritated than might be warranted as Poirot is forced to cope with the silly antics of Miss Stapleton's Ariadne.'

The last of Peter Ustinov's six performances as Poirot was in *Three Act Tragedy* (shown in the UK as *Murder In Three Acts*) which Warner Bros first screened in September 1986. Produced by Paul Waigner, directed by Gary Nelson and written by Scott Swanton, the 105-minute long story was based on the 1935 novel about a retired actor's ill-fated dinner party for thirteen people at which one guest is poisoned. The story itself is notable for having revealed something of Agatha Christie's fascination with the theatre by the way in which she construct-ed the mystery in the form of several 'acts'.

For the movie adaptation, the West Country setting was switched to Acapulco Bay in Mexico – presumably in the hope of an exotic background – but torrential rain during filming unfortunately gave the resulting picture a rather damp look. Even the casting of several famous names, including Tony Curtis, Emma Samms and Lisa Eichorn, could do nothing to enhance the production, which was poorly received on both sides of the Atlantic. *The New York Times*, which had not been openly hostile to the earlier productions, now signalled the death knell on the series:

Peter Ustinov has appeared as Hercule Poirot six times.

'With each succeeding interpretation, Mr Ustinov seems to have become more superficial, relying on assorted tics and mannerisms designed, it seems, to amuse himself as much as the audience. In this latest Poirot caper, Mr Ustinov's performance is one unrelieved 'shtick' from beginning to end... even poor Hastings, who nearly stole the show from Poirot in previous outings, is now kept firmly in the background, trying to look awfully interested while saying virtu-ally nothing.'

It was, in truth, a rather sad end to a series which had begun with such high expectations. Fortunately, though, the character of Poirot was big enough to rise above such set-backs and even before the end of that same year, 1986, he had been restored intact to audiences of both TV and radio...

The disenchantment which Agatha Christie came to feel for Poirot was the inspiration for *Murder By The Book*, a Television South (TVS) special screened on 28 August, 1986. In the hour-long drama produced and written by Nick Evans, and directed by Lawrence Gordon Clark, the Shakespearean actor Ian Holm gave a memorable performance as Poirot.

A precis in *TV Times* outlined the concept of this unusual programme:

Agatha Christie's brilliant detective Hercule Poirot faces the most vital case of his career. A murder is to be committed – and he is the intended victim. His investigation brings him, as night falls, to a splendid but sinister country house... the home of a woman he knows is intent on killing him. What follows is a battle of wits with all the classic ingredients of a Christie murder mystery: a set of Arabian daggers, an old army revolver in a chest of drawers, a bottle of deadly mole poison and a murderous chase along moonlit corridors.

Explaining how he come to devise the drama, Nick Evans said, 'I got the idea after reading a biography of Agatha Christie which mentioned her resentment of Poirot. I began to wonder what might have happened if Poirot had actually met his maker? My imagined confrontation between them was not intended as a send-up, but it does contain a lot of the ingredients which are to be found in Christie.'

Co-starring with Ian Holm were Peggy Ashcroft as the authoress; Richard Wilson (of *One Foot In The Grave*) as her husband Max; and Michael Aldridge as Agatha's literary agent, Edmund Cork. It was a role that Ian relished playing – being a lover of detective fiction and well aware of Agatha Christie's strong feelings about the actors who had played the Belgian sleuth during her lifetime.

'She was not at all happy that all of the men who played him were the wrong size and shape,' he said during filming. 'Poirot was actually quite small, extremely dapper, and with a most elegant moustache. He was certainly not fat. From what I have been told, Agatha could be quite a battle-axe about such things, and Dame Peggy brought that side of her out very well.'

Ian, a diminutive man himself (he is 5 feet 6 inches tall) was certainly not anxious to incur the anger of Agatha's surviving relatives, and modelled his performance very closely on the literary evidence about Poirot.

'I have an oval-shaped head, so that was no problem,' he recalls, 'but to complete the effect I had my hair-line shaved back by three inches. Then I added this impressive moustache and cultivated what I believed to be the correct accent. All in all, it was a fascinating part to play – getting inside one of the immortals of literature is always a challenge, and Poirot is certainly now up there with the very best of them. I'd like to think that Agatha Christie would have approved of my Poirot.'

The newspaper critics certainly enjoyed the production: The *Daily Telegraph* finding *Murder By The Book* 'a fascinating who-dunnit', while Geoff Sutton of the *Daily Mail* had special praise for the star: 'At last – a Hercule Poirot that even Agatha would like.'

Indeed, it is probably true that Ian Holm's performance would today enjoy even greater prominence but for the debut three years later of a fellow Shakespearean actor whose playing of the role has eclipsed all those who went before him...

Christmas Eve 1986 proved another red-letter day for Poirot enthusiasts, when BBC Radio broadcast a ninety-minute adaptation of *Hercule Poirot's Christmas*, based on the 1938 novel about a gruesome murder which Agatha had written as a result of her brother-in-law, James Watts' complaints that the crimes in her stories were 'always too refined and anaemic'. Not surprisingly, she dedicated the original book to him, with a promise that it contained 'good violent murder with lots of blood'!

The BBC adaptation was written by Michael Bakewell, a skilled adapter of mystery stories for the radio, directed by Enyd Williams and starred Peter Sallis as

Ian Holm as Poirot confronts his creator. Agatha Christie (Peggy Ashcroft) in *Murder by the Book*.

Poirot. Among the other cast members were Cyril Luckham as Simeon Lee, Manning Wilson as Colonel Johnson and Edward De Souza as Superintendent Sugden.

Peter Sallis brought a wealth of experience of stage and screen crime to his role as Poirot. For years, in fact, he had specialised in playing villains – on radio in Paul Temple adventures and in television series such as *Public Eye* – before being cast in the role of Clegg in the long-running TV comedy *Last of the Summer Wine*, which is today certainly his best known part. As an enthusiast of Agatha Christie's books, being cast as Poirot was a delight for Peter. In fact he had already worked with several of the actors who had played the little detective, including Albert Finney, Peter Ustinov and Ian Holm.

'Poirot is such a complex and curious man,' Peter says. 'He can be as much of a surprise to listeners as he is to actors, and you are always conscious of having your performance compared to others. At least on radio, though, you don't have to look the part to convince you audience!'

Hercule Poirot's Christmas had one of the biggest audiences on the night of 24 December; and Peter's performance earned him a rave review from the *Daily Telegraph*: 'Sallis's carefully modulated tones without any of the excesses that English actors usually bring to European characters, made his Poirot wholly believable as he went about solving a particularly grisly crime. It was strong fare for the night before Christmas!'

However, like Albert Finney before him, Peter Sallis chose not to repeat his role in the subsequent adaptations which have become something of an annual Christmas treat for radio listeners. in 1987, the old favourite *The Murder of Roger Ackroyd* was the choice for broadcasting, with the versatile John Moffat slipping effortlessly into Poirot's neat little shoes. Michael Bakewell was again the adapter and Enyd Williams the producer.

John Moffat, a dapper man with angular features and a resonant voice, put considerable research into his role, and even posed for publicity photographs in an evening suit, homburg hat and highly waxed moustache! He offered listeners a rather more incisive Poirot than his predecessor. It was a performance he built out of his years as a distinguished stage performer at the Old Vic, the Royal Court and the National Theatre, not to mentions starring roles in two Noel Coward revues, *Cowardy Custard* and *Oh, Coward* which, he says, gave him a real feel for the pre-war era in which Poirot flourished.

'Poirot is very much a man of his time,' John believes. 'He is not obsessed with all the technicalities employed by the modern police force and private detectives. For him the little grey cells are everything

– and that is what I have tried to bring out when playing him on the radio.'

The Murder of Roger Ackroyd was narrated by John Woodvine, with Laurence Payne as Roger Ackroyd and Diana Olsson as Caroline Sheppard. Peter Craze played Inspector Davis and Richard Tate was Inspector Raglan.

Among John Moffat's subsequent broadcasts as Poirot, the highlights have undoubtedly been *Thirteen At Dinner*, *Sad Cypress* and *Murder on the Links*, which was particularly well received. This story also introduced a new Captain Hastings, played by Jeremy Clyde, whose brisk, military-like enunciation contained echoes of another part which he had already made very much his own on the radio – that of Sherlock Holmes.

John Moffat is now probably as familiar to radio listeners as the voice of Poirot as David Suchet has become on television. And the legend which began over sixty years ago when Charles Laughton first strode onto the stage of the Prince of Wales's Theatre in London has reached a new peak of excellence that might finally satisfy the spirit of Agatha Christie.

Also drinking to the continuation of the Poirot legend – Peter Ustinov and Maggie Smith.

AGATHA CHRISTIE'S POIROT

A CHRONOLOGY OF THE LWT SERIES

SERIES ONE

Ten One-Hour Episodes

Produced by Brian Eastman

Executive Producers: Nick Elliott and Linda Agran

Starring; David Suchet, Hugh Fraser, Philip Jackson and Pauline Moran

1. The Adventure of the Clapham Cook

(8 January 1989)

Dramatised by Clive Exton

Directed by Edward Bennett

Co-starring: Brigit Forsyth, Dermot Crowley, Freda Dowie, Antony Carrick, Katy Murphy and Daniel Webb.

The first mystery in the series, in which Poirot investigates the link between the disappearance of a respectable suburban cook and a bank clerk who has absconded with £50,000.

Opposite:
Death in the Clouds
from the fifth series.

2. Murder in the Mews

(15 January 1989)

Dramatised by Clive Exton

Directed by Edward Bennett

Co-starring: Juliette Mole, David Yelland, James Faulkner, Gabriella Blunt and John Cording.

When Captain Hastings makes an idle comment that the noise of fireworks on Guy Fawkes night would provide the ideal cover for a murder he little realises that his Mews garage will soon become the setting for a murder inquiry more complex than the Gunpowder Plot.

3. The Adventure of Johnnie Waverly

(22 January 1989)

Dramatised by Clive Exton

Directed by Renny Rye

Co-starring: Geoffrey Bateman, Julia Chambers, Dominic Rougier, Patrick Jordan, Carol Frazer and Sandra Freeman.

Poirot is called in by wealthy landowner Marcus Waverly to safeguard the security of his 3-year-son, who is under the threat of kidnap. But despite his precautions, the kidnap takes place – and a close relation seems to be implicated.

4. Four and Twenty Blackbirds

(29 January 1989)

Dramatised by Russell Murray

Directed by Renny Rye

Co-starring: Richard Howard, Tony Aitken, Charles Pemberton, Geoffrey Larder, Denys Hawthorne and Holly de Jong.

While dining at his favourite London restaurant, Poirot is intrigued to learn that one of the most regular customers has completely changed his eating habits. The mystery is very much to his taste and leads him on a trail of murder and an ill-gotten inheritance

5.   The Third-floor Flat

(5 February 1989)

Dramatised by Michael Baker

Directed by Edward Bennett

Co-starring: Suzanne Burden, Nicholas Pritchard, Robert Hines, Amanda Elwes, Josie Lawrence and Susan Porrett.

Poirot is disturbed in his flat one night by two young couples who have stumbled across the murdered body of a tenant on the floor below. The police are convinced it is the work of an outsider, but the little detective's suspicions are more centred on the quartet who awoke him.

6.   Triangle at Rhodes

(12 February 1989)

Dramatised by Stephen Wakelam

Directed by Renny Rye

Co-starring: Frances Low, Jon Cartwright, Annie Lambert, Peter Settelen, Angela Down and Timothy Knightly

The 'little grey cells' are resting on holiday in Rhodes when another guest in the hotel is murdered by a poisoned pink gin. Poirot soon finds himself in the midst of a tangled web of love and hate relationships between the assembled guests.

7.   Problem at Sea

(19 February 1989)

Dramatised by Clive Exton

Directed by Renny Rye

Co-starring: Sheila Allen, John Normington, Geoffrey Beevers, Melissa Greenwood, Ann Firbank, Roger Hume and Ben Aris.

Poirot is now on a Mediterranean cruise visiting Alexandria and Egypt. On board is the obnoxious Mrs Adeline Clapperton and all the little detective's senses are put on alert following the remark of a fellow passenger, 'I'd take a hatchet to that woman if I were her husband' – after which she is found dead in her cabin.

8.   The Incredible Theft

(26 February 1989)

Dramatised by David Reid and Clive Exton

Directed by Edward Bennett

Co-starring: John Stride, Carmen Du Sautoy, Ciaran Madden, John Carson and Phyllida Law.

War is approaching, and Poirot goes for a weekend to the home of an aircraft manufacturer developing a new British fighter plane. When the plans are stolen it seems as if they are on their way to Germany – but Poirot suspects the destination is closer to home.

9. The King of Clubs

(12 March 1989)

Dramatised by Michael Baker

Directed by Renny Rye

Co-starring: Niamh Cusack, David Swift, Gawn Grainger, Jonathan Coy, Jack Klaff, Avril Elgar and Sean Pertwee.

Films are of little interest to Poirot, but movie stars are – especially when a visit to Parade Studios thrusts him into a complex case of deception and the killing of an unsavoury impressario. There is also a small professional problem: when is a murder not a murder?

10. The Dream

(19 March 1989)

Dramatised by Clive Exton

Directed by Edward Bennett

Co-starring: Alan Howard, Joely Richardson, Mary Tamm, Martin Wenner, Christopher Saul and Paul Lacoux.

In the final episode of the first series, Poirot is consulted by an industrialist about his suicidal dreams – but the industrialist then dismisses the detective's advice out of hand. But the little Belgian soon discovers that there is more to these dreams than is at first apparent.

SERIES TWO

One Two-Hour Special and Eight One-Hour Episodes

Produced by Brian Eastman

Executive Producer: Nick Elliott

Starring: David Suchet, Hugh Fraser, Philip Jackson and Pauline Moran

11. Peril at End House

(7 January 1990)

Dramatised by Clive Exton

Directed by Renny Rye

Co-starring: Polly Walker, John Harding Jeremy Young, Mary Cunningham, Paul Geoffrey, Alison Sterling and Christopher Baines.

The first feature-length episode of the series opened the second

season of Poirot, with the famous detective and Captain Hastings on holiday on the Cornish Riviera. A chance meeting with threatened Miss Nick Buckley from isolated End House in the bay soon provides Poirot with just the sort of stimulation on which his 'little grey cells' thrive.

12. The Veiled Lady

(14 January 1990)

Dramatised by Clive Exton

Directed by Edward Bennett

Co-starring: Francis Barber, Terence Harvey and Carole Hayman.

Lady Millicent Vaughan calls on Poirot for his help in saving her forthcoming marriage to the Duke of Southshire, which is in jeopardy because of an indiscreet love letter she wrote to a soldier killed in the war. This has fallen into the hands of an unscrupulous character who Lady Millicent fears will show it to her unsuspecting and jealous husband -to-be.

13. The Lost Mine

(21 January 1990)

Dramatised by Michael Baker and David Renwick

Directed by Edward Bennett

Co-starring: Vincent Wong, Richard Albrecht, Anthony Bate and Julian Firth

Poirot explains to Hastings how his 'little grey cells' can also be used to enhance his wealth by clever investments on the stock market. His 14,000 shares in Burma Mines Ltd take on a different complexion, however, when there is talk about the discovery of a new ore deposit, and the only man who knows the whereabouts is soon afterwards found floating in the Thames.

14. The Cornish Mystery

(28 January 1990)

Dramatised by Clive Exton

Directed by Edward Bennett

Co-starring: Amanda Walker, Tilly Vosburgh, Jerome Willis and Derek Benfield.

When a shy and retiring lady comes to see Poirot with tales of getting stomach pains after every meal she eats with her husband – but none when he is away – his interest is excited. The fact that a jar of weed killer has been found half empty and the gardener swears never to have used any makes Poirot realise that he will have to act swiftly to avert a tragedy.

15. The Disappearance of Mr Davenheim

(4 February 1990)

Dramatised by David Renwick

Directed by Andrew Grieve

Co-starring: Mel Martin, Fiona McArthur, Ken Colley and Tony Mathews.

A tour de force by Poirot after hearing about a banker named Davenheim who left his estate to post a letter and has not been seen again since. The little detective promises that he can beat Inspector Japp to the solution of the disappearance – without even leaving his flat.

16. Double Sin

(11 February 1990)

Dramatised by Clive Exton

Directed by Richard Spence

Co-starring: Adam Kotz, Paul Gabriel, Caroline Milmos, Gerard Horan, David Hargreaves, Michael J. Shannon, Amanda Garwood and Elspet Gray.

While Poirot and Hastings are on their way by train to visit old friend Joseph Aarons at Charlock Bay, they meet Mary Durrant carrying a case of valuable minatures to show a client. When these are stolen, Mary implores Poirot for his help.

17. The Adventure of the Cheap Flat

(18 February 1990)

Dramatised by Russell Murray

Directed by Richard Spence

Co-starring: Samantha Bond and John Michie.

Poirot and Hastings decide to lease an expensive flat in an up-market apartment block after the detective's suspicions are aroused. The little Belgian is puzzled as to how two of Hastings' friends, the Robinsons, have been able to rent a flat in the same block for a ridiculously low fee.

18. The Kidnapped Prime Minister

(25 February 1990)

Dramatised by Clive Exton

Directed by Andrew Grieve

Co-starring: Timothy Block, Jack Elliott, David Horovitch, Ronald Hines and Lisa Farrow.

During the last days of the war, the British prime minister is shot at and kidnapped by enemy agents. With a crucial conference about to begin, the government hushes up the affair – but quickly call in Poirot to find the leader before the meeting commences.

19. The Adventure of the Western Star

(4 March 1990)

Dramatised by Clive Exton

Directed by Richard Spence

Co-starring: Barry Woolgar, Bruce Montague, Struan Rodger, Rosalind Bennett, Oliver Cotton, Caroline Goodall and Alister Cameron.

Fashionable society is full of gossip about the remarkable rival sets of diamonds belonging to Lady Yardly and Mary Marvell. But when both these ladies receiving threatening letters, Hercule Poirot finds himself involved in more than society scandal.

ONE HUNDREDTH ANNIVERSARY SPECIAL

20. The Mysterious Affair at Styles

(16 September 1990)

Dramatised by Clive Exton

Directed by Ross Devenish

Co-starring: David Rintoul, Anthony Calf, Beatie Edney, Gillian Barge, Michael Cronin and Joanna McCallum.

The agonising death of the recently re-married owner of Styles Court points the finger of suspicion at most of the occupants of her fine old Essex manor house. Hercule Poirot, a former Belgian police detective, who has recently settled in the village of Styles St Mary is called in to investigate by his friend, Captain Hastings. In the first demonstration of his skills, Poirot reveals the extraordinary power of his little grey cells to expose even the deepest plot. This two-hour special based on Poirot's 1920 debut novel was shown to mark the centenary of Agatha Christie's birth.

Opposite:
Caroline Goodall in
The Adventure of the
Western Star .

SERIES THREE

Ten One-Hour Episodes

Produced by Brian Eastman

Executive Producer: Nick Elliott

Starring; David Suchet, Hugh Fraser, Philip Jackson and Pauline Moran

21. How Does Your Garden Grow?

(6 January 1991)

Dramatised by Andrew Marshall

Directed by Brian Farnham

Co-starring: Catherine Russell, Anne Stallybrass, Tim Wylton,

Margery Masson, Ralph Nossek, Peter Birch and Dorcas Morgan.

A visit to the Chelsea Flower Show where a new rose has been named after Poirot proves to be the beginning of a tricky case of poisoning. The little detective has to travel to Surrey to a home full of Russian orthodox memorabilia to get to the bottom of the affair, which also involves a beautiful young Russian emigre.

22. The Million Dollar Bond Robbery

(13 January 1991)

Dramatised by Anthony Horowitz

Directed by Andrew Grieve

Co-starring: Oliver Parker, Natalie Ogle, Ewan Hooper, David Quilter, Paul Young, Lizzy McInnerny and Kieron Jecchinis.

When the joint General Manager of the London and Scottish Bank is nearly killed by a hit-and-run driver just before he is due to sail on the maiden voyage of the Queen Mary, Poirot is told it must be a case of attempted murder. But when his enquiries take the little detective to sea, he needs all his skills of detection as well as a strong stomach to unravel the facts.

23. The Plymouth Express

(20 January 1991)

Dramatised by Rod Beacham

Directed by Andrew Piddington

Co-starring: John Stone, Marion Bailey, Alfredo Michelson, Shelagh McLeod, Julian Wadham and Kenneth Haigh.

A visit from Ebeneezer Halliday, an Australian magnate, who is worried about false rumours concerning his Yellow Creek group, is only the beginning of a complex case for Poirot. Events take a further twist with the unexpected arrival of Halliday's daughter's estranged husband, demanding money, which is followed swiftly by murder.

24. Wasp's Nest

(27 January 1991)

Dramatised by David Renwick

Directed by Brian Farnham

Co-starring: Martin Turner, Melanie Jessop, Peter Capaldi, Kate Lynn-Evans and John Boswall.

An innocent case of a tea-leaf reading at a garden fete becomes painful for Poirot when he is inadvertently stung by wasps. While purchasing some iodine at a local chemist, he catches a glimpse of the register of poisons as well as an incriminating photograph of a pretty fashion model, and is soon in the midst of a case of attempted murder.

25. The Tragedy at Marsdon Manor

(3 February 1991)

Dramatised by David Renwick

Directed by Renny Rye

Co-starring: Ralph Watson, Ian McCulloch, Geraldine Alexander, Anita Carey, Desmond Barrit and Neil Duncan.

When Poirot is summoned urgently to a country hotel to solve a

murder and finds that the landlord is a crime writer seeking a solution to a difficult plot, he is not amused. But the arrival of a mysterious stranger and the discovery of a body soon get the little grey cells working at full stretch.

26. The Double Clue

(10 February 1991)

Dramatised by Anthony Horowitz

Directed by Andrew Piddington

Co-starring: Kika Markham, David Lyon, Nicholas Selby, Charmian May, William Chubb, Michael Packer and David Bamber.

A spate of unsolved robberies brings Inspector Japp to seek Poirot's help. When a well- known jewellery collector holds a party and loses a valuable emerald necklace the little detective is soon on the trail – but a woman from his past complicates a difficult case still further.

27. The Mystery of the Spanish Chest

(17 February 1991)

Dramatised by Anthony Horowitz

Directed by Andrew Grieve

Co-starring: John McEnery, Pip Torrens, Antonia Pemberton, Caroline Langrishe, Malcolm Sinclair and Peter Copley.

Duelling and rivalry are at the heart of this mystery in which Poirot himself is a witness to the murder of Arnold Clayton whose body is found in a chest. Although the little detective's own life is put under threat, he manages to expose a cunning plot with his usual aplomb.

28. The Theft of the Royal Ruby

(24 February 1991)

Dramatised by Anthony Horowitz

Directed by Andrew Grieve

Co-starring: Nigel Le Vaillant, John Vernon, Frederick Treves, Stephanie Cole, David Howey and Tariq Alibai.

International relations are put at risk when a drunken young Egyptian prince has a priceless ruby stolen from him in a restaurant. Although Poirot is soon able to recover the missing gem, he has more difficulty exposing the culprits and their real motive.

29. The Affair at the Victory Ball

(3 March 1991)

Dramatised by Andrew Marshall

Directed by Renny Rye

Co-starring: Mark Crowdy, David Henry, Andrew Burt, Nathaniel Parker, Haydn Gwynne, Kate Harper and Natalie Slater.

When Poirot attends a Ball, he quickly senses two noblemen who are studiously avoiding one another despite their known friendship – then one of them is found dead with a table knife through the heart. A book in the dead man's possession provides the clue which eventually enable the detective to unmask a cunning killer.

30. The Mystery of Hunter's Lodge

(10 March 1991)

Dramatised by T.R.Bowen

Directed by Renny Rye

Co-starring: Roy Body, Bernard Horsfall, Jim Norton, Diana Kent, Shaughan Seymour, Victoria Alcock and Clare Travers-Deacon.

While attending a grouse shoot, Poirot catches a cold and has to retire to his hotel bed. In his absence one of the guests is shot, and the detective has to rely on Hastings and Inspector Japp to do his legwork before he can reveal all at a dramatic gathering in Hunter's Lodge.

SERIES FOUR

Three Two-Hour Episodes

Produced by Brian Eastman

Executive Producer: Nick Elliott

Starring: David Suchet, Hugh Fraser, Philip Jackson and Pauline Moran

31. The ABC Murders

(5 January (1992)

Dramatised by Clive Exton

Directed by Andrew Grieve

Co-starring: David McAllister, Allan Mitchell, Cathryn Bradshaw, Michael Mellinger, John Breslin, Nicholas Farrell, Nina Marc and Donald Douglas,

A mysterious letter signed only with the initials 'ABC' which challenges Poirot to show just how clever he is at solving mysteries seems like a hoax to Inspector Japp. But when a shopkeeper in Andover is found murdered with a copy of the ABC Railway Guide open beside her body, the little detective at once realises he is not on the trail of a crackpot but a clever killer.

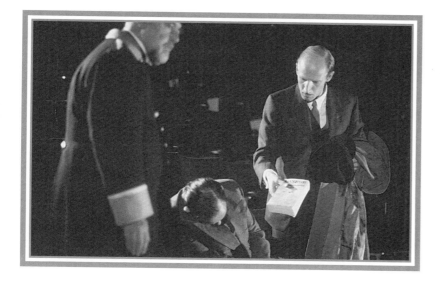

32. Death in the Clouds

(12 January 1992)

Dramatised by William Humble

Directed by Stephen Whittaker

Co-starring: Sarah Woodward, Shaun Scott, Richard Ireson, David Firth, Cathryn Harrison, Amanda Royle, Eve Pearce and Jenny Downham.

A routine flight from Le Bourget to Croydon is only unusual because of an aggravating wasp that has to be killed and then the discovery just before landing that one of the passengers, a woman, is dead. When a blowgun dart is discovered, Poirot is the only detective who can possibly discover how someone could have been killed in a closed compartment in full view of all the other passengers.

33. One, Two, Buckle my Shoe

(19 January 1992)

Dramatised by Clive Exton

Directed by Ross Devenish

Co-starring: Carolyn Colquhoun, Joanna Phillip-Lane, Peter Blythe, Chris Spicer, Michael Tudor Barnes, Alan Penn, Guy Oliver Watts and Joe Greco.

After a visit to his dentist, Henry Morley, Poirot is surprised to be telephoned later the same day by Inspector Japp with the news that Morley has been found dead, apparently having killed himself. Once on the case, however, the detective begins to suspect that this is not a case of suicide – all the more so when he runs through the list of other patients who sat in the dentist's chair on that fateful day.

SERIES FIVE

Eight One-Hour Episodes

Produced by Brian Eastman

Executive Producer: Nick Elliott

Starring: David Suchet, Hugh Fraser, Philip Jackson and Pauline Moran

34. The Adventure of the Egyptian Tomb

(17 January 1993)

Dramatised by Clive Exton

Directed by Peter Barber Fleming

Co-starring: Peter Reeves, Bill Bailey, Paul Birchard, Jon Strickland, Olivier Pierre, Simon Cowell-Parker, Mozattar Shafeie and Rolf Saxon.

Sir John Willard, the famous archaeologist, has discovered the tomb of King Men-her-Ra in Egypt, but at the moment of his triumph when he opens the sealed burial chamber he suddenly has a heart attack and dies. Because Sir John's widow has reasons for suspicion about the nature of her husband's death, she calls in Hercule Poriot, who soon finds himself confronted by two more deaths and the suggestion that a terrible ancient curse is at work...

35. The Underdog

(24 January 1993)

Dramatised by Bill Craig

Directed by John Bruce

Co-starring: Bill Wallis, Andrew Seear, Denis Lill, Ian Gelder, Jonathan Phillips, Adie Allen, Ann Bell and John Evitts.

A mysterious fire at the chemical factory of Sir Reuben Astwell, where a new compound called Astroprene is being developed which is followed by the murder of Astwell, brings Poirot into a tangled web of espionage and commerce. Miss Lemon helps her employer to get to the bottom of the mystery by using her powers of hypnotism on Lady Astwell, who recalls a stranger talking to her husband not long before his death.

36. Yellow Iris

(31 January 1993)

Dramatised by Anthony Horowitz

Directed by Peter Barber-Fleming

Co-starring: David Troughton, Geraldine Somerville, Hugh Ross, Stefan Gryff, Yolanda Vasquez, Arturo Venegas and Joseph Long.

A visit to a newly-opened French restaurant in London brings back memories for Hercule Poriot of a killing in Buenos Aires two years earlier. When the same group of people who were involved in the previous death by poisoning again reappear in the London restaurant and another person dies, Poirot finds himself sifting the clues and finally uncovering the links between the two murders.

37. The Case of the Missing Will

(7 February 1993)

Dramatised by Douglas Watkinson

Directed by John Bruce

Co-starring: Mark Kingston, Terence Hardiman, Rowena Cooper, Edward Atterton, Gillian Hanna, Beth Goddard, Susan Tracy and Neil Stuke.

When Poirot and Hastings attend a debate at the Cambridge Union on equal rights for women, they find themselves drawn into a family dispute and a plan by one of the speakers, Andrew Marsh, to change his will. When Marsh is found dead later in the evening having been called away to an old folly in a wood, Poirot suspects that there are skeletons in the family cupboard which he will have to uncover to explain the mystery.

38. The Adventure of the Italian Nobleman

(14 February 1993)

Dramatised by Clive Exton

Directed by Brian Farnham

Co-starring:David Neal, Anna Mazzotti, Sidney Kean, Vincenzo Ricotta, Leonard Preston, Janet Lees Price and Arthur Cox.

After Poirot and Hasting's dinner date is interrupted to go to the scene of another evening meal which has been brought to a sudden end with the death of the host, Count Foscatini, and no sign of his guest, the little grey cells are instantly on the alert. Hints of a Mafia-type organisation, the Masnada, warn Poirot that he is on danger-ous ground, with high finance and blackmail at the root of the problem.

39. The Chocolate Box

(21 February 1993)

Dramatised by Douglas Watkinson

Directed by Ken Grieve

Co-starring: Rosalie Crutchley, Anna Chancellor, James Coombes, George Whitehead, David de Keyser and Jonathan Hackett.

On a visit with Inspector Japp to his old stamping ground, Brussels, Poirot is suddenly reminded of a case which he apparently failed to solve over twenty years earlier. This concerned a poisoned box of chocolates and the honour of a beautiful woman – the combination of which provide the clues to Poirot's seemingly odd actions.

40. Dead Man's Mirror

(28 February 1993)

Dramatised by Anthony Horowitz

Directed by Brian Eastman

Co-starring: Zena Walker, Richard Lintern, Iain Cuthbertson, Fiona Walker, Emma Fielding, Tushka Bergen and Jeremy Northam.

An Art Deco mirror which Poirot fails to buy at an auction leads

him to the home of the purchaser, collector and dealer, Gervase Chevenix. When Gervaise is later found dead in his study with a gun in his hand, a whirlpool of family emotions as well as an inheritance become the focus of the little detective's enquiries.

41. Jewel Robbery at the Grand Metropolitan

(7 March 1993)

Dramatised by Anthony Horowitz

Directed by Ken Grieve

Co-starring: Trevor Cooper, Sorcha Cusack, Hermione Norris, Karl Johnson, Elizabeth Rider, Simon Shepherd and Arthur Cox.

While Poirot and Hastings are on holiday in Brighton, a new play opens entitled *Pearls Before Swine* in which the leading actress wears a magnificent pearl necklace that had once been given to another famous actress by the Tsar of Russia. When this goes missing from a locked box, Poirot is charged with finding the necklace, which is essential to a planned American tour, and soon finds himself in the middle of what may well not be theft, but a huge insurance fraud.

SERIES SIX

Four Two-Hour Episodes

Produced by Brian Eastman

Executive Producer: Sarah Wilson

Starring: David Suchet, Hugh Fraser, Philip Jackson and Pauline Moran

42. Hercule Poirot's Christmas

(1 January 1995)

Dramatised by Clive Exton

Directed by Edward Bennett

Co-starring: Mark Tandy, Catherine Rabett, Simon Roberts, Brian Gwaspari, Sasha Behar, Eric Carte, Andree Bernard and Ayd Khan Din

Just as Poirot is settling down for a quiet Christmas, he is summoned to the country mansion of Simeon Lee, a rich, bitter old man who believes his life is in danger. When Lee sets up a fake telephone call to his solicitor to change his will in the hearing of his relatives – and is shortly afterwards found with his throat cut – Poirot has to abandon all thoughts of a merry Christmas and track down a brutal killer.

43. Hickory Dickory Dock

(17 February 1995)

Dramatised by Anthony Horowitz

Directed by Andrew Grieve

Co-starring: Paris Jefferson, Jonathan Firth, Damian Lewis, Granville Saxton, Gilbert Martin, Sarah Badel, Rachel Bell and David Burke.

A series of thefts at a student hostel are only the beginning of a case which plunges Poirot into a murder committed with morphine nitrate and the events of the Jarrow march. The finger of suspicion points at Sir Arthur Stanley, the champion of the marchers, but another tragic murder and then hints of smuggling have to surface before Poirot can solve the mystery.

44. Murder on the Links

(Autumn 1995)

Dramatised by Anthony Horowitz

Directed by Andrew Grieve

Co-starring: Bill Moody, Damien Thomas, Jacinta Mulcahy, Bernard Latham, Ben Pullen, Diana Fletcher, Terence Beesley, Sophie Linfield and Kate Fahy.

Shortly after Paul Renauld consults Poirot about being defrauded by a group of Chileans, he disappears and his body is found with a love letter initialled 'BD' in a pocket of his coat. when Poirot sets out to unmask the killer he finds himself investigating the events of a murder that took place ten years earlier as well as an unscrupulous case of blackmail.

45. Dumb Witness

(Autumn 1995)

Dramatised by Douglas Watkinson

Directed by Edward Bennett

Co-starring: Patrick Ryecart, Kate Buffery, Norma West, Julia St John, Paul Herzberg, Ann Morish, Pauline Jameson and Muriel Pavlow.

When Poirot and Hastings arrive at Lake Windermere to watch Charles Arundel break the water speed record, they are immediately informed by the Tripp sisters that they have had a supernatural warning that Charles' aunt, Emily, is in danger of her life. When Emily is found dead, the Tripp sisters hold a seance to try and learn who the killer is – but once again Poirot relies on his famous little grey cells to uncover a clever plot involving deception and a disputed inheritance.

Agatha Christie Society

President
Rosalind Hicks

Vice Presidents
Joan Hickson
David Suchet

Chairman
Mathew Prichard

Joint Editors
Corinne Pitts
Elaine Wiltshire

Address
P O Box 985
London
SW1X 9XA

If you have enjoyed this book you may be interested to know about the Agatha Christie Society.

The Society was formed in March 1993 to promote communication between the many and loyal fans of Agatha Christie and the various media who strive to bring her works to the public.

The Agatha Christie Society is run under the auspices of Agatha Christie Limited, so we can guarantee that all the information you receive through the Society has been gathered by those people who have a commitment to and love of Agatha Christie.

Members receive four newsletters a year, each one packed with information about Agatha Christie. There are interviews with the personalities who have brought Agatha Christie's characters to life on the stage and screen; behind-the-scenes aspects of filming; publishing worldwide; listings of where you can see productions of Agatha Christie plays and much, much more.

These newsletters are very much a two-way operation, and many of the articles are written by members from around the world.

Meetings are arranged from time to time to give members the opportunity to gather together and exchange information about their favourite writer.

If you would like to become a member, please write to The Agatha Christie Society, PO Box 985, London, SW1X 9XA.